The True Church

A STUDY
(*Historical and Scriptural*)

By
ALLEN MACY DULLES, D. D.
*Professor of Theism and Apologetics in the Auburn
Theological Seminary*

NEW YORK   CHICAGO   TORONTO
Fleming H. Revell Company
LONDON   AND   EDINBURGH

New York: 158 Fifth Avenue
Chicago: 80 Wabash Avenue
Toronto: 25 Richmond Street, W.
London: 21 Paternoster Square
Edinburgh: 100 Princes Street

PREFACE

THIS book is but an argument. It makes no pretense to furnish information concerning The Church, which may be found in such admirable works as those of Hatch and Hort and T. M. Lindsay, representing the evangelic notion of The Church; or the more recent works of Darwell Stone and Durell, representing the Anglo-Catholic opinion.

The substance of the book was given as lectures to the students of the Auburn Theological Seminary and it is published to meet in some measure the need of any who may wish to see some of the facts concerning The Church arranged so as to be better able to answer sophistical questions such as, " who has authority to give sacred bread" (A. J. Mason); and the constantly reiterated statement that in order to have authority " from above" a minister must be in supposed apostolic succession.

It is a criticism of the catholic position of which Gore and Moberly have been such ardent defenders, that The Church has been from the beginning a society with a divinely appointed succession of those who are in " holy orders."

The author feels that the churches are in danger today of returning to an ecclesiasticism which has, in the past, limited Christian liberty and corrupted Christian service.

The criticism of ecclesiasticism of the catholic kind is keenly pointed by Oman ("Faith and Freedom," p. 322), "The Person of Jesus loses all real significance as soon as we interpret Him mainly as the Founder of an outwardly authoritative institution."

Ritschl wrote in 1859 (*Studien und Kritiken*) "There is need of this apologetic justification of the evangelic concept of The Church because false determinations or measures of what The Church is are to-day current within evangelical Christendom."

There is not less need to-day.

A concept of The Church which excludes the Quaker, Fox; and the leader of the Salvation Army, William Booth; must be, can be, shown to be false.

This is our purpose, to state and defend the evangelic concept of The Church, not to show that any one form of church government is better or worse than another.

While the author would have gladly given time, if he had had it, to make his little book more perfect, both as to matter and form; and to remove defects of which he is probably as conscious as any reader; yet such as it is, he dedicates it to the service of The Church which is, indeed, the Bride of Christ, and to the churches which are the existence-centres of that Church on earth, in the hope that the churches may more and more come to a unity of faith and hope and love, and so to an outward unity free from inner antagonisms.

Auburn, N. Y., November, 1907.

CONTENTS

8   Contents

I

THE TWO CONCEPTS OF THE CHURCH

Religion is necessarily social.
This is particularly true of the Christian religion.
The name for the Christian association is, Church.
The content and concept of the word Church has varied.
There are two concepts, evangelic and catholic.
In what respect these differ.
The catholic concept.
The evangelic concept.

I

THE TWO CONCEPTS OF THE CHURCH

WHILE religion is a personal and individual matter, in that it is the response man gives to the God whom he recognizes in his world, yet it is true of almost every form of religion that it is associational.

What is called, rather vaguely, the religious instinct is a social instinct.

Few individuals would, if they could, be solitary religionists. While there is that in religion which may cause man to be alone with his God at times, yet no religion could propagate itself except as it caused the association of its adherents with one another. We take it for granted, then, that religion is the affair of an association, of a society of people. That this is true of the religion called Christian is beyond question. True, some have sought to be Christian in isolation. But, this is contrary to the genius of this religion which has as one of its supreme commandments, the love of the brethren. From the beginning, when Christ made disciples, those who believed in Jesus were associated together. Of this we have such full evidence in the New Testament that it is not necessary to examine the matter.

No one can doubt that the Christian, as was its mother religion, the Hebrew, is of all religions preeminently social, since it makes the religious bond the chief means of union whereby its members are united. The slow but sure effect of the Christian religion is to dissolve all national ties.

This association of Christians has almost from the very start been called ecclesia or church. The Church has been corporate or institutional Christianity.

It would have been a blessing of immeasurable value if a pure doctrine or belief concerning The Church had prevailed from the earliest to the present time. Unhappily, hardly a century after Christ we see the beginning of a struggle between two ideas or concepts of The Church which has lasted till to-day with sad results to The Church. It is clearly evident to any who look at all attentively at the adherents and advocates of the Christian religion that these are divided among themselves into two distinct parties.

There are two and only two distinct concepts of The Church. There may be Christians and churches not clearly self-classified, not accurately placed, yet every Christian and every church is either " catholic " or " evangelic."

We use these two terms as most convenient and historically most accurate. We might say " catholic " and " reformed "; but since the non-catholic idea is, in our opinion, the older, injustice is done in calling the non-catholic idea " reformed." As " catholic." is a self-appropriated name by one division of Christians we do no injustice to them in so naming them, though in so doing we must say at once that there is no concession of exclusive right to its use. Nor does this linguistic concession mean, as Cardinal Gibbons maintains, that the later self-styled catholic church, the Roman Church, is alone catholic in the ancient sense of this word.

The representatives of these two do not differ as to the general importance and necessity of churches for the existence and propagation of the Christian religion but they do differ as to the seat of the authority which may pertain to this association as well as the nature and extent of that authority.

They differ as to the exact nature of the mission which is given to Christians as a Church.

They differ as to the means and methods whereby The Church should execute the trust committed to it.

They differ also as to the relative position of Christ, Church and Christian.

The evangelic and catholic concept of The Church differ, concisely stated, in this: The evangelic notion is that the Christian religion, the Christian conscious-ness forms and determines Christian churches which all manifest The Church. The catholic notion is that there exists a formally established society which, as a Church, forms and determines the Christian religion. So Schleiermacher, concisely differentiates: in Protes-tantism The Church is reached through Christ, in Catholicism, Christ is reached through the Church.

In the catholic concept, The Church, it is supposed, can and does exist only in one form, which is essential not to its mere well-being, but to its very being, and the true religion is that which this church has, it is said, maintained, still teaches and always will teach.

That this is a correct statement appears from the insistence upon apostolic succession, of some sort, in all catholic churches. It is maintained that The Church had an *existence form from Christ*. The society which Jesus is supposed to have established has, as essential to its existence, those who perpetuate in some way of outward succession the authority which, these maintain, was given to it by Jesus Christ.

The catholic concept is: The Church is an institution created by Jesus Christ, to which He has given His own authority and power, and this authority and power are present in some form of government. This governing body is supposed to be of Christ's own appointment, existing by His will, representing His authority, embodying His spirit. It has "the keys" for the government of The Church and of the world. This governing body can declare what doctrines are divinely true and obligatory on man. It can determine what man's religious and even secular duty is. From the third century until the fifteenth, this was the prevailing concept; for a thousand years this was practically the only thought or idea of The Church.

Catholicism has existed under various forms, and, though these parts contradict one another in other matters, and even as to the seat of authority, yet all parts of the catholic church agree in the assertion that the authority which is derived from the Spirit of God, the presence of Jesus Christ resides in the episcopal or other so-called heads of The Church.

In the catholic notion, The Church is existent only in a society which has a divinely determined form of government. Its visibility is secured through divinely determined ordinances, administered by those whose appointment originated with the first appointed officers of The Church by Jesus Christ. Divine grace is received through visible sacraments, according to a divine arrangement, so that redemption or salvation is communicated by outward and visible means. Christ's words, " as My Father hath sent Me, even so send I you," which is supposed to mean the apostles and their successors, is the charter of its existence and transmitted authority. It has power and right to bind on earth and in heaven. An Anglican bishop has defined The Church as, Christians *under the rule of bishops*, successors to the apostles. " The catholic conception of the bishop, secures the channels of grace and truth and represents the Divince Presence " (Gore, " The Church and the Ministry," p. 61). The extreme form of the catholic concept is expressed in the Douay Catechism definition of The Church, as " the congregation of the faithful under Jesus Christ, their invisible head, and His vicar on earth, the Pope."

The reformed or evangelic concept of The Church is that this word Church names the whole body of God's children, of whom Christ is Saviour and head. It is the " general assembly of the Church of the first-born."

This Church of the redeemed, the true Israel of God has no perfect existence in visible organized form or unity on earth. But, this Church of God, purchased with " His blood" is manifest and apparent in the many churches. The churches manifest The Church.

So Paul says: " The Church of God which is at Corinth."

A church is a society of the children of God which includes a certain number of those who outwardly profess the religion of Jesus Christ, and who publicly practise it. The Church is present wherever two or three are met in Christ's name. The Church is one and undivided, because the indwelling Spirit of Christ is indivisible. It may have no outward unity, which the world can see, but there is one life in every part. Within The Church, *as it appears to man*, there may be those who, Judas-like, are not vitally of it. The Lord knoweth them that are His.

The reality of The Church is not affected by the presence of incongruous elements within a church. The True Church may attract some who are not spiritually born again.

The Church exercises the functional activity assigned to it by Jesus Christ, through the ministry of the churches as each member is animated by His Spirit.

The Church is perpetuated and propagated by means of the Word of God. No fixed outward form is necessary for its existence. This Church has no " Holy Orders" except such as man forms and so names, for expedient purposes, and none that are essential to its being. All Christians, as Church members, are holy. The " Sacraments " pertain to the growth of the Christian character and are expedient to the verge of necessity for the visibility of The Church, yet we cannot deny that the Quakers are as truly a church as are the Roman Catholics, so far as they unite in Christian worship. It is now out of the question that the whole Church meet in one place at one time and there declare its doctrine or opinion; and no part of The Church can represent the whole with authority as possessing the Spirit of God. Even the first great Church council (Acts 15) passed resolutions which did not bind the whole Church. Congregations, assemblies, councils, conclaves, speak for themselves alone, and their utterances are opinions and are not divine doctrine, and these may err. The assent of the whole Church is necessary that any decree of a part of the Church shall be regarded as Church doctrine. There is no absolute " quod semper, quod ubique, quod ab omnibus."

As the whole Church cannot meet in one place, and no part of The Church can equal the whole, no part has power to include or exclude from communion with the whole Church, nor from God. · Savonarola and Luther were not excommunicated from the whole Church, only from a part of it. The part speaks for the part and not for the whole. Any part of The Church may recognize those as *its* ministers who appear to themselves charismatically prepared for its service. Any part of The Church may express *its opinion* as to what is divine doctrine and what is for godliness. The *final truth* of such declarations is dependent on the immediate fellowship with God of those who utter them, but in nowise can these utterances be made obligatory upon others except as these are voluntarily received as true by others in their own consciousness.

The doctrines and ordinances of a church are obligatory only upon the voluntary members of such a church. Every association of Christians recognizes Truth and recommends it according to its condition of inspiration. God alone is Lord of the conscience, and to God not to a church is every Christian responsible.

Religious truth is not known otherwise than scientific truth. The difference between scientific and religious truth is not the method of apprehension, but what is apprehended. The catholic churches, however, claim immediate inspiration. These claim to be inspired, God-filled with a divine power to discern and declare truth.

The protestant churches while dependent upon God, as are all who seek truth, yet claims no exemption from fallibility and human means.

Between the "inspired" catholic church and the fallible, yet truth-loving protestant churches, there can be no common ground.

An association of such as agree among themselves because of personal persuasion that they have reliable knowledge of religious verities, and these who accept truth as revealed through the or a church, claiming infallibility, cannot agree.

There is no via media, as Cardinal Newman found. Thus there are two churches, as there were two Israels. As the Israel of old, an outwardly organized, priestly institution was the existing Israel in the sight of the world, yet not the Israel of God's election; so any existing church, recognized as such in the world, in virtue of some ecclesiastical organization, is not *The Church*, not what Jesus called " My church." So, says Paul, there are two Jerusalems.   There is a church " which answereth to Jerusalem, which now is, and is in bondage with her children," and there is a Church which is like " the Jerusalem above, free, the Mother of us all."

II

THE REPRESENTATIVES OF THE TWO CONCEPTS

———

There are separate representatives of these concepts.

1. The Catholic : Roman.
   The Catholic : Orthodox (Greek).
   The Catholic : Chaldæan.
   The Catholic : Syrian.
   The Catholic : Gregorian.
   The Catholic : Coptic.
2. The Evangelic : Lutheran.
   Reformed.

II

THE REPRESENTATIVES OF THE TWO
CONCEPTS

THESE two conflicting concepts of The Church
have each numerous representatives. We shall first
briefly notice those churches which represent the
catholic concept. In passing, it is worth while noting
that there is no power in this concept, as is sometimes maintained, to preserve a visible unity in The
Church of God. The bitterest antagonisms of Christendom have been among catholic churches.

1. The representatives of the catholic concept.

(1) Chief among them is the church which calls
itself the Holy Roman Catholic Apostolic Church.
This church claims the two great apostles, Peter and
Paul, as its founders. It relies chiefly upon the
primacy of Peter among the Twelve for its own primacy
and supreme authority. This church fell heir to the
power and the glory of the name of Rome, and has
perpetuated its world-ruling spirit, and is the legitimate heir of that mighty power which once ruled the
world from the city on the seven hills, by the Tiber.

The extinction of the churches of North Africa
removed what might have been a rival, as Carthage
was to ancient Rome. The practical annihilation of
the British churches (See Green's " History of England"
and Kurtz, " Church History ") and the general accept-

ance of the rule of Rome in the North put this church
in complete supremacy in all Western Europe, a
supremacy it maintained until the great outbreak of
the liberal spirit in the sixteenth century, called the
Reformation.

(2) Almost equal to Rome in its magnificence
and power and rivalling it in its pride and self-suffi-
ciency, is the Holy Oriental Orthodox Catholic
Apostolic Church, commonly called the Greek
Church.

This church prides itself on its Apostolic origin,
on its preservation of a true succession, on its perpetuation of the original orthodoxy of The Church.
It represents itself to be the continuation of the true
Christianity. It glories in being of Greek origin.
It boasts itself of the use of the apostolic language.
Christianity, said Napoleon, was the triumph of Greece
over Rome. This church claims to be the continuation of this triumphant Christianity. It is catholic;
it has divine authority; it is orthodox; it is apostolic.
Its seat of authority was Constantinople, the city
built by the far-seeing sagacity of Constantine, which
remained the capital of the Roman Empire for a
thousand years after Rome fell. It is still the capital
of the Greek church. This church exists in two
affiliated branches: one under the direction of the
œcumenical patriarch at Constantinople; the other
under the control of the Holy Synod in Russia.

(3) There are in the East other churches, which
claim to represent the catholic concept of The Church.
There were Christians in Damascus before Paul was

converted to the Christian faith. Those of "the Way" scattered themselves all over Syria. The East-Syrian or Chaldæan church, later called Nestorian by its enemies, was an extensive congregation of Christians in the second century. Edessa, in Mesopotamia, was the seat of the authority which governed this church. Abgarus VIII (A. D. 176–213) was favourable to the new religion. It spread far over Asia. Its missionaries penetrated into China and went as far south as Ceylon. But it was finally overwhelmed in the Moslem tide which spread over the East. Its destruction was hastened by bitter feuds and contentions. Its clergy was often corrupt. A brief period of prosperity, under the Turkish rulers, favourable to it because this church was antagonistic to that of Constantinople, has been succeeded by a lethargic, unspiritual, deathlike condition.

(4) The Syrian church, in the West, rivals the Chaldæan in antiquity. It also claims Peter as its founder, and certainly with more reason than Rome can show. But, whoever was its founder, it is sunk deep in superstition and its light is buried beneath a mass of ritualism, so that it resembles little that ancient congregation at Antioch which sent forth Paul and Barnabas on the first great missionary tour, and which presented, at the beginning, such a noble example of what the True Church is. It has separated into two divisions : one is that ruled over by the Jacobite patriarch who always bears the name of Ignatius; the other, the Maronite division, since the crusades, has been in nominal union with Rome.

(5) As early as the days of Tertullian (died 220
A. D.), Christian communities flourished in Armenia.
These suffered terrible persecution in the latter part of
the third century. This church was rescued from extinction by the extraordinary labours of Gregory the
Illuminator, after whom the church is named the
Gregorian (not the Armenian) church. He succeeded
in the conversion of the king of Armenia (302 A. D.).
Succession in the patriarchate is maintained by the use
of his dead hand,—fit, if mournful, symbol of the dead-
ness which has fallen upon this church as a whole.
This is the most numerous of the Oriental churches,
except the Græco-Russian, from which it is separated
on account of some trifling credal difference, due, it is
said, to the accidental absence of its bishops from the
Council at Chalcedon (451 A. D.).

(6) The Christian church in Egypt was once
mightier than either the church at Rome or Constantinople. To-day it is reduced to two shrunken rem-
nants.

(a) The Coptic church is a remarkable monument
of Christian antiquity. The Copts are the descendants
of the ancient Egyptians. The patriarch resides at
Alexandria, once the chief among Christian cities.
He alone has the right to ordain, which he does by
breathing on the one to be ordained, without the imposition of hands.

(b) The Abyssinian church was planted from Alexandria and rapidly spread over Ethiopia and into
Nubia. This church is remarkable chiefly for its ad-
herence to Old Testament customs. It observes the

Sabbath as the sacred day, and practices circumcision. There is an annual baptism day when the sins of the people are washed away, as on the old Day of Atonement. Pilate is regarded as a saint, because he washed his hands in innocence of the blood of Christ. Its canon of scriptures includes eighteen patristic writings.

2. While the churches called protestant, born of the great Reformation, generally present the evangelic concept of the church, yet there has not been wanting, at times, a very pronounced catholic tendency. Much of "protestantism" has been merely a protest against some other form of "catholicism." This has appeared chiefly in the "catholic" claims made by some in the Anglican and the affiliated Episcopal church in America, by a large part of their clergy. To give an example: Bishop Doane, of Albany, N. Y., said (in New York *Independent*, Feb. 3, 1887): "Our priesthood is representative of Christ, and has authority to act for Him," and he affirms the duties of the priest to be that of "offering sacrifices and of absolution." Among other urgent representatives of this catholic conception, we shall have occasion to mention Bishop Gore and the late Canon Moberly.

The evangelic concept of The Church has come into force and being with the Reformation. Though Luther receded from his original position, made fearful by the excesses of those who confused license and liberty, and though Calvin laid emphasis on The Church as an organization, yet the notion was reborn that The Church was the whole people of God, irrespective of ecclesiastical organization or outward authority, and that all authority was in the Holy Spirit, and Jesus Christ the only Head of The Church. This evangelic element has been the strength of protestantism. "Springing up in secret struggle, it is matured by thought, watered by personal experience, and rooted directly in God. It has been the child of conscience, the pupil of philosophy, the companion of poetry, the parent of freedom" (R. H. Hutton, "Essays"). To the present day, the evangelic concept has hardly had adequate recognition, although represented in the reformed churches. The Quakers were too positive in their negations, tending to make *no government* a *mark* of The Church, and the Salvation Army does not call itself a church. But, under the influence of progressive thought, the evangelic concept of The Church is slowly, yet surely taking possession of the genuinely reformed churches, while those churches claiming to be catholic are tending more and more to one prevailing type, that of the Roman Catholic church.

The catholic concept has had influence in both the Calvinistic and Lutheran churches, yet it has not dominated these churches. The seat of authority has been too uncertain to permit of any authority, whether congregational or presbyterial, becoming more than declarative, advisory, monitory. A declaration of faith by a Congregational Association or a Presbyterian General Assembly, is not more than an expression of opinion. " All councils may err." What a Presbytery, or any number of Presbyteries, may decide is but the opinion or belief of those voting for such decision. It does not express the mind of those not declaring themselves. In these churches the individual is free. There is no coercion. The only arguments are appeals to the understanding of the revelation of God's truth. Those who differ may be excluded from fellowship, may be treated as heretics, may be ostracized, but there is no attempt to exclude from God's Church nor from salvation. Excommunication is a mere announcement of separation which has practically taken place, with no physical force supporting it, between the individual and a particular church, which speaks and acts for itself.

The churches of the Reformation are practically representatives of the evangelical concept, only here and there some writer or some assemblage may assume a tone and use language, as though divinely directed and empowered to say or do some particular thing.

The churches of the Reformation can indeed glory in their work, and, as representatives of the evangelic concept, testify to its truth and to the fact of the divine favour.

It is an absurdity when Cardinal Gibbons says, "the Protestant churches, even taken collectively, are too insignificant in point of numbers and too circumscribed in their territorial extent to have any pretension to the name catholic." They may not pretend to the name "catholic," but this is not because "protestant" churches are insignificant either as to quantity or quality.

Protestantism, through protestant nations, has far more influence in the world to-day than has catholicism.

It is enough for the glory of the Reformation and the evangelic concept of The Church, that we point to what The Church, as represented by the reformed churches, has done in Germany, in France, in England, and in Scotland and America, and in its missions throughout all the world.

It is also undeniable that the catholic churches themselves have become purest, and most serviceable to mankind in lands where the evangelic concept of The Church has held sway.

That catholicism is healed by evangelicalism, is itself a demonstration of the superiority of the latter concept of The Church.

What has the catholic concept achieved, in making the catholic churches superior blessings to the nations of the East, or to the people of Italy, or Australia, or Spain, or Ireland, or wherever dominant as in Mexico and South America?

III

THE ANGLICAN CHURCH

The peculiar position of the Anglican Church.
Catholicity not originally claimed.
Anglicans quoted : Cranmer, Fisher, *et al*.
The criticisms of a Roman Catholic.
The evangelic elements of the Prayer-Book.
The Anglican Church has broken succession.
Its history is recent.
The British Church.
The Anglican Church a secession.
The catholic claim an obstacle to unity.

III

THE ANGLICAN CHURCH

THE position occupied by the Anglican church is peculiar. It has within it both a catholic and an evangelic tendency. The former is perhaps the stronger, at least more pronounced, to-day, claiming that the Anglican is the truly catholic Church.

Concerning this claim, put forth by a party in the Episcopal Church in England and America, it must be immediately noted that it is a party and not a church claim.

Dr. Schaff says : (" Creeds of Christendom," Vol. I, p. 607), "The Church of England has never officially and expressly pronounced on the validity or non-validity of non-Episcopal orders. The Thirty-nine Articles are silent on the subject, though Bishop Burnett says that the wording of the Articles on church and ordinances was expressly selected for the exclusion of the idea that apostolic succession was requisite to the valid dispensation of the sacraments."

That is to say, the Anglican church does not claim that the ministry and the service of this church are of direct appointment from Christ, but are a matter of human arrangement; not, of course, excluding the operation of the Holy Spirit upon individual minds and hearts.

Cranmer asserted the parity of bishops and presbyters, and sought to bring to pass a general council to

frame a concensus doctrine. To unchurch the other
protestant churches was a thought which never entered
Cranmer's mind. Writing to Calvin, he urges that harmony of doctrine will tend to unite the Church of God.

Fisher said that "A prelate like Whitgift had no
disposition to find fault with the foreign protestant
churches for the lack of episcopacy."

Hooker contended, despite his belief that episcopacy
had prevailed since the time of the apostles, that there
may be sometimes very just and sufficient reasons to
allow ordination without a bishop. That reason, he
admitted, was valid in the case of the foreign churches.

When Laud first declared that there could be no
church without a bishop, he was reproved by the Oxford authorities, because he cast a bone of contention
between the Church of England and the Reformed on
the continent.

In 1647 Bishop Hall said in his Irenicon, "Blessed
be God, there is no difference in any essential between the Church of England and her sister Reformed
churches. The only difference between us consists in
our mode of constituting the external ministry. And,
even with respect to this point, we are of one mind,
because we all profess to believe, that it is not an essential of the church, though, in the opinion of many,
it is a matter of importance to her well-being."

Hall, though himself a pronounced defender of episcopacy, again says, "The foreign churches lose nothing of the true essence of a church, though they miss
something of their glory and perfection," without episcopacy.

. Usher and Baxter desired a modified episcopacy.

As lately as 1903 the Bishop of Durham wrote in the *Contemporary Review* that he was " distinctly with " Canon Henson in his " powerful appeal for the frank recognition, as churches, of the non-Episcopal societies, such as the Methodists " ; for " I know," he said, " that however boldly modern manuals may tell us that ' no Bishop, no Church,' is a primary Christian truth, that tenet was denied by such Anglican Bishops as Andrews, Hall, Usher and Cosin, to name only those four names out of well-nigh the whole succession of our greatest Churchmen from the Reformation onward till within quite modern times." In the same review more recently the Rev. Dr. Rashdall, Fellow of Oxford, described the theory of apostolic succession as a " gigantic figment." (See also in his " Christus in Ecclesia.")

In an article in the *Presbyterian Review* (Vol. IX, p. 35), Dr. Welch (of Auburn Seminary) cites Jewell, Field, Stillingfleet, and of course Whateley,—as rejecting high church claims for Episcopal ordination.

In this article, he quotes Bishop Fleetwood as saying, " We had many ministers from Scotland, from France and from the Low Countries, who were ordained by presbyters only and not by bishops, and yet were never reordained."

A statute of Queen Elizabeth requires those who had received non-Episcopal ordination to subscribe only to the Articles of Religion, and did not exact reordination.

In fact, it would be hard to find any one of the

Church of England who in those days thought of calling in question the validity of the order and sacraments of the Reformed churches.

Perry ("History of England," Vol. I, p. 19) says, "At first, all that was contended for was, that episcopacy was permissible and not against Scripture." (See also Blakeney "Book of Common Prayer," 1870.)

In addition to those already named, the great Andrewes expressly disclaimed the necessity of Episcopacy, and Cosin freely communicated with the French Reformed church during his exile. Indeed, it is not until the latter half of the past century, that more than a relatively small minority of English churchmen have been committed to a claim which, unhappily, was made in part as a counter claim to the divine right of presbytery.

As Dr. Sanday has written, " It should be distinctly borne in mind, that the sweeping refusal to recognize the non-Episcopal Reformed churches is not and can never be made, a doctrine of the Church of England; too many of her most representative men have not shared it."

Archbishop Tait's words are well-known, " He could hardly imagine there were two bishops on the bench or one clergyman in fifty who would deny the validity of Protestant clergymen solely on account of their wanting the imposition of hands." Not only is the catholic pretension opposed within the Anglican church itself, it is also vehemently denied by both the Greek and the Roman Catholic Church. The refusal of the Roman church to recognize Anglican orders, on the ground of lack of intention is well taken from a catholic viewpoint.

Apostolic succession is not sufficient to establish the high church claim. Hutton says ("Anglican Ministry," p. 28): "A church is not apostolic simply by the possession of a true episcopate. The possession of orders does not constitute a church." There must be *intention* so to perpetuate the church.

He charges against the Anglican, that the Anglican priest knows nothing of the supernatural powers of a sacrificing priesthood, that the priest is "either a sacerdotos or layman, there is no middle place."

The Roman Catholic church declares the Anglican priest is but a layman. The "Catholic Church" does not and cannot forget that the attitude of the Anglican church, in the beginning, was distinctly protestant.

Upon this point history is clear and decisive despite the efforts strenuously made, especially in America, to repudiate this Protestantism. The Anglican church can never get away from its past history.

Even Hooker regarded the pope as anti-Christ. "Mass" was denounced from every pulpit, and in its place was the "communion." The "altar" became the "table." The Prayer-Book shows positive intention to destroy all belief and devotion connected with the "catholic" sacrifice at the altar.

Penance was repudiated. Intercession of the saints is regarded as profane. Confession is granted merely as a sort of concession to some weak ones.

Indeed, the protestant character of the Articles and the Prayer-Book is too apparent to be disputed.

The endeavour was to get rid of " Roman superstitions."

As Hutton says (o. c., p. 182), "The primitive
Anglican ministers of Parker's ordination loathed the
very notion of the office of the mass-priest, and would
have died rather than have had it conferred upon
them." To be ordained a "catholic" priest was, for
years, a capital crime in England.

Says *The Catholic World* (quoted: Hutton, o. c.,
p. 170)," We see with what an unerring sacrilegious
instinct everything bearing upon the holy sacraments,
and even upon the holy presence, is either cut out or
peiverted in the Anglican ordinals."

" The bishop and ordinands explicitly profess their
disbelief in the sacrifice of the mass, and they signed a
document wherein it is described as a blasphemous
fable and a dangerous deceit" (Hutton, o. c., p. 183).

There is thus the evident, deliberate intention to exclude the doctrine of the sacrifice from the communion, although this doctrine is sometimes maintained by the Episcopal clergy.

The absolution is simply the declaration by the
ministry of God's word, and is not anything else than
that which any man might declare. As Hutton says,
" It is such a declaration as would be made by a boy
in the ' Catholic Church.' "

Absolution is simply a last resort for those who
ought to have been able—so the Prayer-Book implies
—to quiet their consciences without it. This is not a
mark of a church possessing a sacerdotal ministry.

The Anglican priesthood is commissioned to remit

sins, only in terms which require no sacerdotal character at all.

The interchangeableness of the words priest and minister in the Prayer-Book is very significant of the intention to get rid of the sacerdotal character of the priesthood, as is also indicated by the rejection of the term, altar. In the act of ordination, a prayer is used which is evidently not to confer sacerdotal power.

The duties of a bishop are described in terms that are not sacerdotal. He is to administer, discipline, teach, preach and feed. He is not in any sense a high priest.

When a priest is ordained, it is in these words, " Be thou a faithful *dispenser* of the Word of God and of His holy sacraments."

In the communion, as the Anglican Prayer-Book says, the priest stands before a table and not at an altar; and, in his prayer, the sacrifice of Christ is purposely declared to have been once for all complete; and the communion is simply " a *perpetual memory* of His precious death and sacrifice"; and those who commune are commanded to " take and eat this in remembrance that Christ died for thee, and feed on *Him* in thy heart by *faith*," which absolutely excludes any thought of sacrifice in the " catholic" sense, and is simply a protestant, Calvinistic communion.

Although many Anglicans have deplored the influence of Calvin in the Prayer-Book, that influence is there, and can never be got out of it.

Whatever may be said by the eager high church-

men of the Episcopal church, sacramentalism and
sacerdotalism are still new in the Anglican church,
and struggle hard to maintain a place in it, in oppo-
sition to the plain teaching of the Book of Prayer.

There are a few hundred ritualistic churches, in not
more than a dozen of which is the new mode of worship, " five and twenty years old," and these serve to
bring out in stronger relief the protestantism of all the
rest, and, indeed, of all until our own day (see Hutton,
o. c., p. 20).

The attitude of the Prayer-Book towards sacerdotalism of the " catholic " sort is not a question of lethargy,
but of fierce denial. The Reformation was a violent
outburst of anti-sacerdotalism. The Greek and the Roman churches have, therefore, with consistency rejected
the claims of this party of the Anglican church. There
is but one way for an Anglican " priest " to enter the
Roman Catholic priesthood, that is, as any other layman must. This, not a few have done.

From an historical point of view the Anglican
Church is a schismatic church. It separated itself
just as really from the mother ecclesiastical organization as did the other Calvinistic churches. The Anglican church was, of course, Calvinistic.

The succession of its ministry or priesthood, which
came from the Roman Catholic church for a thousand
years, was broken when, under Henry VIII this
church declared itself separate from the papacy. In
consequence of this division this church came under
the anathema of the Roman Catholic church.

When Henry VIII became king, there was no

bishop, priest or deacon in England whose ordination was not through Roman channels.

The Church of England, as a distinct church, had no existence before the year when that separation took place. Before that date it had been simply the Roman Catholic church in England. " Rome is the hole of the pit whence, spiritually, we were digged," very frankly says A. J. Mason, Professor of Divinity, Cambridge (" Principles of Ecclesiastic Unity," p. 107).

Before that date, the Anglican church had no more existence as a church than the United States existed before its Independence was declared, secured and definite government established. As the colonies then became independent of the English Constitution, so the Anglican church became independent in the reign of Henry VIII.

There were Christians and a Roman Catholic church in England, but there was no Anglican church before Henry VIII. " The English Church is the daughter of Rome," says A. J. Mason (Op. cit., p. 107). Therefore, it cannot be said that *the present* Anglican church is not the offspring of the Roman Catholic church, but of the old British church. This is repeatedly stated by high church Episcopalians who ignore the facts. A recent writer says, since the British church refused to unite with the Roman church under Augustine, " this shows that Augustine and his forty monks did not establish the English church." But this writer fails to notice the consequence of this refusal on the part of the old British churches. *They were annihilated.* This is the testimony of every

competent historian, whether secular or religious.
Kurtz (" Kircheng," § 77) has sketched this total
destruction.

Richard Henry Green, in his " Making of England,"
has also described this conflict, and Prof. A. V. G.
Allen, in an article in the " Dictionary of Religious
Knowledge," states the effect of the complete destruction of the old British church.   Therefore, all notion
that the present Anglican church derives its succession
from the old British church must, from an ecclesiastical
viewpoint, be abandoned.   For a thousand years the
Church in England was Roman Catholic and nothing
else.

There is but one way by which the Anglican can
get back to the apostles, and that is through the
Church of Rome.   But this way, as we have said, is
completely barred by the fact that the Anglican church
is a broken off branch, and is cast away by the Church
of Rome.   Its ministers are all laymen, so its mother-
church declares.

That a bishop can retain power to ordain when in a
schismatic state, no high church Anglican would pretend.   If three bishops could carry succession from the
apostles, simply by the fact of their going through a
form of ordination, any one sees that there might be
hundreds of little churches started, each one of which,
however thoroughly schismatic, would be a " catholic "
apostolic church.   Such, for example, is the Reformed
Episcopal church in the United States.

*Seceders, on the high church principle, lose their
original church rights;* on the protestant principle

they do not; but on the " catholic" principle, secession nullifies the power of ordination, and the
papal conclusion is logically correct, the Anglican
church has no " catholic" ministry. So Rome has declared with reiteration.

It is greatly to be regretted that the Anglican
church, and the American daughter, are not willing to
occupy the position to which history assigns them, as
Reformed churches. This is where their best scholars
place them, from Hooker and Hall, to Sanday and
Rashdall. No other one thing would do more for the
union of all the churches, and the emphasis of the
evangelic concept of The Church than the return of
the whole Anglican church to its original ecclesiastical
position, as in the days of Usher and Baxter and
Andrewes and Jewell.

To this desirable end a correct concept of the True
Church will greatly contribute.

The errors have not been all on one side. The dis-
senting churches in England have done much to
hinder any fellowship by calling harmless practices
sinful and through inability to discern that a true concept of the Church leaves large liberty both in the way
of a ritualistic service, as well as in a non-ritualistic
way.

IV

WHY SEEK TO DECIDE WHICH CONCEPT IS VALID

What the catholic claim includes.
Its magnitude and potential dangers.
The catholic churches have wrought good.
They have wrought evil.
The difference as to the evangelic churches.
The healthfulness of the latter.
The inseparableness of church and religion.
The possible dangers of religion.
The tyranny of religious leaders.
The potency of religion for evil.
The requirement that authority be demonstrable.
Every Christian desires to belong to the Church.
If the only church is the " catholic."
Dean Stanley quoted. Tertullian's dictum.
The divisions of Christendom and need of unity.
The question is forced on us continually.
Episcopal claims in America.
The doctrine of Church concerning itself fundamental.
The matter cannot be left to self-solution.
" Laisser faire " lets the vociferous prevail.

IV

WHY SEEK TO DECIDE WHICH CONCEPT
IS VALID

THERE are not a few Christians who fail to appre-
ciate the importance of ascertaining what The Church
truly is. Many acquiesce in error because, they say,
it makes little difference what one thinks about The
Church,—the one essential matter is, what one thinks
about Jesus Christ.

It is obvious that this indifference is almost exclusively limited to those called protestants, and therefore this indifference works steadily for the growth of
the catholic claim.

The catholic claim, whether made in the interest of
papal, episcopal, or perhaps presbyterial church government, includes the matter of the salvation of the
individual soul, as well as the advance of the rule and
dominion of Jesus Christ, because the Catholic church
is thereby made the ark of salvation.

Those who carelessly encourage the growth of the
catholic concept do not realize all which this claim
involves. It is a claim fraught with consequences
which have, alas, so often been most ruinous to Christendom and to the spiritual progress of the religion of
Jesus. Consider what an awful claim it is, this, that
men are clothed with the authority of God Himself,
are the infallible voice of His Spirit, the visible channels through which alone grace and salvation come to

mankind, through the so-called sacramental actions as means of grace. We do not question that the catholic churches have often nourished a celestial life and guarded in secret the riches of piety. They have kept before man his eternal destiny and the dread realities of the unseen world.

We do not deny, but gladly recognize that The Church when the catholic concept ruled has produced a vast amount of good among men. The Church, even when mostly catholic, has never completely buried the cross, not altogether obscured the gospel. We recognize that The Church, when most exclusively under catholic dominion, patronized the arts which ennoble life with culture and refinement. We cheerfully admit that in this catholic church some of the world's most precious treasures have been preserved as in an ark amid the storm and stress of dark ages.

Yet no one can dispute with reason that this same church, under the persuasion of its inherent right and authority from Jesus Christ through the apostles to save men, as it represented the matter to itself, has been guilty of deeds which would shame the most barbarous period through which man ever passed. No association of men, in the pursuit of any goal has ever equalled the cruelty and atrocity which has had its defense and justification in the assumed fact that some part of The Church has divine authority, inasmuch as it is catholic, episcopal, papal. That the churches calling themselves catholic have used their assumed authority tyrannously cannot be denied.

Against this church it must be charged that it has

bribed and blinded man's conscience and perverted his notions of right and wrong.

In the execution of its purposes, the catholic church has availed itself of every kind of influence and force whereby to constrain and compel man into an outward, if not an inward, accord with itself. When it has seemed desirable, the catholic church has imposed a yoke of ignorance on man, that his credence might not be disturbed by the light of truth. She has encouraged superstitions and the practice of heathen customs, in order that the doctrines she taught might be rendered acceptable to the natural man. She has antagonized science in its search after knowledge, and, on the plea of the utility of religion, has conserved the errors which have become incrusted in the religious consciousness.

Believing religion to be the most important of all human concerns, and the religion of the catholic church as the only true religion, the catholic church has claimed and exercised the right to subordinate to religion every other human concern. In the theoretical interest of the soul, and of this church as the Kingdom of God, the catholic church has assumed and asserted authority over every vital function, whether individual or social, and has regarded any means as justified which seemed in the interest of the catholic church and her work.

The limit of human ingenuity has been reached in devising and exercising the most refined or brutal tortures wherewith it is possible to bring anguish to man's body, mind or spirit. Te Deums have been sung, and rejoicing prevailed, when massacres and treacherous assassinations have been carried into execution. Thousands and tens of thousands have been given over by the church power to the abuse of cruel hordes engaged in the falsely called crusades, whereby the Cross has again been covered with the sacrificial blood of the saints of the Most High who loved not their own lives.

The catholic church has dissolved all human relations, for her own increase in power, and for the effecting of a religiousness which the church desired to promote. The obligations of man to live and to speak the truth to his neighbour, to keep faith with his fellow man, were nullified on the principle that the highest end justified all means and made them good. The church has, for its own purposes, fanned human passions into a flame, rulers have been aroused against their subjects, and subjects against their rulers. She has now favoured despotism and again has encouraged insurrection and anarchy. She has sown the seeds of dissension and let loose all the horrors of war. The church has enslaved man's conscience, dictated policies to governments, cast her yoke over the populace, assumed the control of man's religious emotions, determined his creed, directed his conduct, and even claims to settle his eternal destiny, with power to leave him in, or deliver him, from purgatorial pains, and even to doom to an everlasting hell.

It is not to be wondered at that the catholic church and its religion have been too often hated. The evil is not because she is organized, but *because of her self-*

delusion that this organization is divine in authority and power, whence a species of madness has come upon those who imagine their opinions and actions to be those of God Himself, and every conceivable excess has been committed to the harm of mankind and the shame of The Church of Christ, in the name of the Christ who declared to the would-be persecutors, James and John: " Ye know not what spirit ye are of."

It is not to be denied that this delusion of divine authority has at times taken possession of some protestant communions. But it was contrary to the spirit of the Reformation and has been repudiated as contrary to the spirit of the Christian religion with almost no exceptions among present reformed churches.

It is not maintained that the evangelic churches have been unmixed blessings, since each and all have erred most grievously both in practice and in precept. But, the evils which the evangelic churches have wrought against truth and righteousness are incidental to the human composition of the churches and are not involved in the idea that any church is infallible or is divinely directed. The evangelic concept does not permit the deification of error. Though at times evangelic churches have assumed that they were possessors of divine truth and have leaned towards the catholic idea of an inspired, divinely directed church, yet this has been so far an abandonment of the evangelic concept, and is simply a further illustration of the danger which is potential, if not always actual, in the catholic concept.

It cannot be successfully denied by any who study history that the evils which lurk in the catholic notion of The Church are lessened in force wherever the evangelic concept has power.

In Protestant lands, as in England and America, the Roman Catholic church is acknowledged to be purest and best in the matter of the character of priest and people. It is quite evident and undeniable that the danger of self-corruption which lurks in the catholic concept is arrested to some degree by the healthful influences of the evangelic, free and liberal concept of The Church and its religion.

The power of any Church for good or evil can only be understood when we remember that a church is organized religion, with all the potency of religion over the lives of mankind.

Religiousness is a permanent characteristic of man. The immensity of the world fills him with wonder. The measurelessness of life generates yearnings after the unseen, the intangible. Nature awakens various and bewildering emotions. Hopes and fears alternately possess man under the influence of the phenomena amid which he lives. That civilization or scientific education will ever materially change man and make him actually irreligious is incredible. Knowledge tends to deepen and quicken the emotions and convictions we call religion. Positivism itself must take a religious form if it will live. When M. Guyau proclaims and would prove, the " Irreligion de l'Avenir " the impression he and others make cannot be extensive nor permanent. For, God has or-

dained that the phenomenal world shall cause man to
" feel after Him." Knowingly or ignorantly man will
continue to worship God. So far as he does not
possess the reality, he will fashion an image. Science
may affect religion, but will never extinguish it.
Science makes the world more and more wonderful.

The permanency of religiousness among men, does
not secure that every form of religion is an unmixed
blessing. If in religion man has found ground for
hopes, he has also found material for despair. Not
seldom religion has given man fearful visions by day,
and dreadful dreams by night. As Lucretius well
said: " quantum religio potuit suadere malorum."

As religion is an affair of human nature, however
divinely touched, it may, and often does make evident
the basest elements of human nature.

In religion man's strongest passions are influenced,
whether good or evil. Man's gladness and his sad-
ness, his love and his hate, his purity and his sensuous-
ness, his hope and his despair appear alternately in religion. If the influences we term religious have glori-
fied man, they have also at times debased him. The
crimes committed in religion's name are more in number and more devilish in kind than those committed
in the name of liberty. Religion has been as a fire, the
flame of which has burned clear or dark, according to
the fuel it has found. While, like a stream, it has
sometimes cleansed the channels through which it has
passed, yet it has too often itself become corrupted
from the region through which it has flowed, and
carried poisonous matter to bring death to those

drinking in the hope that this was the pure river of the water of life.

There is no other form of tyranny which is so easily established as the tyranny of the priest who assumes religious authority. There is no other form which has been so fruitful of horrors. A concept of the Christian Church which asserts this tyranny of a priesthood, of an episcopacy, of a papacy should be examined with more care than ever was the divine right of kings. Whoever pretends to represent God and speak with His authority must have credentials beyond any doubt.

Besides the desire to deliver the mind from error and tyranny there is also in every true Christian a desire to be associated with other Christians within what may be truly called in the New Testament sense The Church.

The genuine Christian desires to belong to, be in association with, those who, like himself, are heirs of salvation; that is, he desires to belong to, be a visible member of, The Church of God.

This he desires because the Church of God is His covenant people, the number of those whom Jesus Christ, as the Captain of Salvation, is leading to glory.

Not to belong to this Church, as it is visible in the unitedness of God's children, in separatedness from the world, through fellowship of faith and life, is, so far as it is willful, a contradiction that one is a child of God, and therefore a cutting off of one's self from the blessings God has for His people.

If the evangelic churches are not manifestations, and colonies, so to say, of God's people, if the only church is that which answers the catholic concept, then the Christian must join himself to this—if he can find it. There can be no conceivable religious gain, rather loss, in association with a company of people who are not God's people, not a part of the ecclesia of God.

If it is essential not merely to the *well*-being, but the *being* of a church, that it be " catholic," then we must accommodate ourselves to this fact.

But, if what is *called* catholicity be no essential, and the essence of a church is that it is a company of those who are disciples of Christ, then this fact established leaves the great multitude of evangelicals, the many millions, still in the Church of God, and not only concedes them the blessedness of Church, that is, covenant fellowship, but it makes union between all such churches possible, because all are but parts of, or rather manifestations of, the One Church.

As Stanley says (" Eastern Church," p. 25), " If the Christian religion be a matter, not of mint, anise and cummin, but of justice, mercy and truth; if the Christian Church be not a priestly caste, or a monastic order, or a little sect, or a handful of opinion, but the whole congregation of faithful men dispersed throughout the world; if the very word which of old represented the chosen ' people ' (*laos*) is now found in the ' laity ' ; if the Biblical usage of the phrase ecclesia literally justifies Tertullian's definition : ' *ubi tres, sunt laici, ibi est ecclesia*,' then the true Christian need not worry him-

self over the problem as to which particular church is
The Church."

The unity of Christendom demands the settlement
of this question concerning the nature of the Church.

How desirable this unity is, is a common theme of
to-day.

The differences and frequent antagonisms which
mark the relation of Christian associations, called
churches, is a sore evil under the sun.

Christendom is more divided religiously than it
is politically, and often the factions are more intensely
hostile.

A divided Christendom cannot hope to conquer
heathendom. Division, so far as it is antagonism,
postpones indefinitely the day when the kingdoms of
this world are to be the Kingdom of God and His
Christ. "We might easily convert even Turks to the
gospel if we agreed among ourselves" (Cranmer).

Hostility among Christians is a scandal to unbe-
lievers, being a virtual negation of claims of Christ.
Few subjects are so persistently presented to the
Christian public as the desirability of unity.

The unity of Christendom must be by the universal
acceptance of *either* the catholic *or* the evangelic
definition of the Church. It is incumbent on the
evangelical Christian either to prove his position or
else accept the catholic. This means, that the
evangelical must show the truth of his own, and therefore the erroneousness of the catholic definition of
The Church. All Christians must either come under
the dominion of the catholic church, or else all

churches must be recognized as manifestations, however imperfect, of God's Church, so far as they are
associations of God's children, worshipping the Father
in spirit and in truth.

To the question *how* any churches are to be recognized as God's Church, we answer at once that it
is not by means of outward signs, for the preaching
of the word and the right administration of the sacraments are not outward signs; churches are, as true
Christians are, spiritually discerned.

There are some who regard the disunion of Christendom as doctrinal rather than governmental. But,
far more than many realize, agreement concerning
other doctrines depends on agreement concerning the
doctrine as to The Church.

That which affects most powerfully doctrinal differences in the Church is the *question of authority*.
The question which creates the widest difference is,
whether the true religion, the religion of Jesus Christ,
is to be determined by a church or recognized by the
sanctified reason of the Christian community. The
notion which some entertain, that there is a third
possible mode of determination of doctrine, by means
of the Bible, is contradicted by the fact that the
Bible, as any other book, conveys truth only as it is
interpreted rightly, either by a church inspired for
this purpose, or by the community of Christians
guided, according to reason, by the divine light.

The settlement of the question, whether a church
is this authority, or whether the individual must ascertain religious truth for himself, it may be in as-

sociation with and helped by others, dependent upon the Spirit of Truth, precisely as any other truth is acquired, is of primary importance.

That it is a question, in some respects *the* religious question of the day, is constantly forced on our attention. For example we have this recent public utterance, as reported in the *Tribune* (New York) May 16, 1907.

" Disbelief in a priesthood and the sacramental system, in the opinion of Bishop Worthington, is the insurmountable obstacle to Christian unity. The bishop discussed the subject in his annual address, which was read before the council of the Protestant Episcopal diocese of Nebraska to-day.

" ' Christian unity,' he said, ' is to be desired. There is nothing that can be said reverently and wisely to sustain an argument in favour of sectarianism in Christianity. The failure to secure unity is due to the disbelief in the Protestant world in a priesthood and the sacramental system which this involves. Until there is the acceptance of this teaching of the Bible and prayer book there can be no organic union among Christians. Concerning this vital question no concession can be made.' "

Another, if older, illustration is furnished by Bishop Doane, of Albany, N. Y., who wrote in New York *Independent*, Feb. 3, 1887: " Our priesthood is representative of Christ, and has authority to act for Him," and he affirms the duties of the priest to be that of " offering sacrifices and of absolution."

Recently, a publishing house put out a book,

"The American Church," that is, a history of the Protestant Episcopal Church in America. This claim is more and more frequently made. The ministers who call themselves "priests" boast of peculiar powers and rights which they say are from Christ through "apostolic succession." Fortified in this belief, they refuse fellowship with other ministers and unchurch all other churches. To be a "churchman" is more than to be a Christian, to be catholic is more than equivalent to being a child of God.

The real unity of Christendom demands that such claims be examined, and if false be refuted and the truth set forth. Until this question is decided there can be no unity. Men will hesitate between the two. The maintenance of either disturbs those who hold the other opinion.

It is, therefore, as related to our religious knowledge and our belief, that the question of *The Church* becomes of first importance. Is there, or is there not, a church which is the all exclusive and inclusive depository of truth and grace, which is, as a visibly organized body, the sole source, the only channel, of religious knowledge: or, is The Church larger than any church, including all those who in some form of association recognize Jesus as Lord and maintain Christian fellowship?

The problem of problems for The Church is, first,— *itself*. When this is clearly solved, and the conclusion accepted, then and then only will the differences between those who are truly God's children begin to be settled. Until there is agreement as to The Church, this difference of opinion will affect belief as to every other doctrine, as faith in the teacher affects the faith of the taught.

It might be said, that the settlement of this question can be safely left to the growth of true religion in the human heart, that the true Christian spirit will pay no attention to such matters as church government, that larger ideas are rapidly transforming bulwarks into boulevards, that fraternization takes place despite ecclesiastical ostracism. This is so, and we are thankful that it is, yet the truth as truth has some rights and makes demands for its vindication. Christian unity is greatly assisted by the breaking down of the ecclesiastical barriers. It is worth having in mind that the fellowship of protestant Christians is far more real than between protestant and catholic, or even among the separated so-called catholic churches. The antagonism of the Greek and Roman churches and the Anglican has no parallel among Protestant churches to-day.

We must also reckon with the fact, when we would pursue the laisser faire process, that human nature is so weakly constituted that claims, irrespective of their actual worth, are accepted among men according to the positiveness and perpetualness of the assertion of their truth. Persistent repetition is, for the larger part of mankind, the one guarantee of truth. It is not an altogether dignified parallel, yet it is a parallel to the assertion by this or that body of Christians that it is *The* Church when we say that the advertisement that " Royal Baking Powder is alone pure " is worth millions to the company making it, for precisely the same

reason that many are persuaded that the so-called
" catholic" churches are alone churches. " If it is not
an Eastman, it is not a Kodak," is precisely like what
is said by some Christians, and with the same effect,
that many accept the assertion as true,—" if it is not
Episcopal, it is not a church." That Pears' soap has
special cleansing power is so impressed on the Anglo-
Saxon imagination by continual representation, that
multitudes would think themselves unwashed if it had
not been used.

We must regard this frailty of human nature, and
the ease with which assured assertion is regarded as
equivalent to proof when a church claims that it is
" *Catholic*" or " The *True* Church."

Imperious claims, though supported by force, or by
appeals to the emotions and the senses, cannot be admitted to be true unless sustained by ample reasons.
Certainly this high-church claim to be representative
of God in any infallible way cannot be conceded short
of absolute demonstration.

We must consider and decide whether such demonstration is at hand.

So far as any charge of partisanship in presenting
the protestant side, it may be said that the catholic
never hesitates to urge his own peculiar view, and
therefore cannot find fault when the protestant does
likewise.

The Anglo-Catholic partisan must also remember
that the evangelical who disputes his conclusion, is
doing no more, often not so much, as the most learned
and devout members, bishops and others, of his own

church. The evangelic concept of The Church finds support within the Anglican Church through such men as Lightfoot and Hatch and Hort and Sanday and Bruce and Brown and Westcott and a host of others, leaders in their Church.

For the reasons named, it seems to be our duty, as Dr. Rashdall has said (" Christus in Ecclesia," p. 121), to contend for the simple truth concerning the Church. He says : " I believe that the doctrine of the Apostolic Succession is one which it is right to preach against, because it is an obstacle to Christian Unity and Christian Charity."

V

THE DIFFICULTIES

There are difficulties.
Assumption that some form is necessary to the Church.
Charles Hodge quoted.
The successful church as The Church.
Timidity.
The personal equation.
Macaulay on progress in religion.
Superstitions have hold on many.
The longing for peace.
The rest in authority.
Manning's frank expression.
Indifference to truth.
R. H. Hutton's criticism.
J. H. Newman's attitude.   Brunetierfe.
The desire for the bishop.
Influence of forms.
The church as an organization and salvation.
Bishop Gore quoted.
The evangelic disposition.
The supremacy of rational truth.
The Church the fellowship of believers.

V

THE DIFFICULTIES

THERE are many difficulties in the way as we seek the true concept of The Church.

We have alluded to the indifference which causes many to ask, what is the use? Assisting this " let alone " state of mind is the fact, the churches which represent an extreme opinion do so much good, present ecclesiasticism so magnificently, that any one who sees danger to-day, as in the past, in the growth of ecclesiastical despotism, is a troublesome alarmist.

There is difficulty, because so many who are indeed interested in the truth do not weigh the force of their admissions. For example, a professor in a Presbyterian Seminary writes, " The Church must receive some form of external organization." Such an opinion may easily lead to the conclusion that, if *some form is necessary*, then the form must be fixed and final in some church now existing, for, inevitably, if some form is necessary, The Church must have had some external organization from the beginning.

Contrary to this, Charles Hodge says: " The Church might exist in scattered believers," and he remarks that Calvin would have been surprised, if any had maintained that visible organization is necessary. (See "Church Polity," p. 73, and elsewhere.)

Too many fail to discern the fallacy in the reasoning

that because government is necessary to the *well*-being of *a* church therefore it is necessary to the *being* of *The* Church.

Many are carried away with the notion that *a church* which governs its members most successfully is *The Church* with a divine government.

Many are caught by the sophistical sentence : No man can make himself a Christian minister. Upon this one sentence alone (constantly reiterated in one form or another), it may be said, the whole structure of Anglican high-churchism is erected. We shall need to examine it. Here it may be simply said, that because no man can make himself a Christian minister the conclusion cannot be drawn, that some other man or class of men, can.

Many fear that if the concept of The Church as a society which has no necessary government were to gain sway, that religious anarchy would result, and too timid to trust to the Spirit of God, they prefer to entertain the concept, regardless of graver consequences, that The Church received a form of government from Jesus Christ.

In fact, in all this most momentous matter, the minds of the people are more influenced by fancies than by facts, by fears than by reason, by indolence than by industry, with no small measure of self-interest cast into the balance. Because, the clergy, whose own authority is at stake, and who have many selfish reasons for maintaining their divine right to rule in the house of God, are constantly busy persuading others as well as themselves that The Church cannot exist without fixed government, and that they, the clergy, constitute this government.

The greatest difficulty lies in the personal equation. Therefore, before entering on the further consideration of the problem we are considering, it will be worth our while to estimate the value of the personal equation, the subjective element, which enters into the determining of this matter.

We must estimate the work of two differing, and even contradictory, tendencies, each of which may be deeply rooted in human nature.

How deep and how strong the catholic concept is, Macaulay illustrates when he said that the " catholic " church " may exist in undiminished vigour when some traveller from New Zealand shall in the midst of a vast solitude take his stand upon London Bridge to sketch the ruins of St. Paul's."

Macaulay could not see any progress in religious history. " During the last seven centuries the public mind of Europe has made constant progress in almost every department of secular knowledge. But in religion we can trace no constant progress." On the face of it, this is unreasonable, that the human mind should allow any essential matter of human thought to escape from that scrutiny and consequent knowledge which has characterized its progress in other departments of human thought.

Yet, Macaulay but gives extreme expression to a fact. The difference between the catholic and evangelic, protestant Christian is deep rooted, and the uprooting of the catholic idea will be slow. There are those whose feelings dominate their reason, whose perception of truth and their valuation of it is second to their perception of beauty and their valuation of peace and repose of mind.

Probably all are timid to a greater or less degree, and fear to let what is called reason enter into the sanctuary of faith. Almost every one has a sacred region to which he admits his reason, if at all, only under guard.

If all our superstitions could fall as harmlessly as fell the great and beautiful Campanile at Venice, few would resist so violently as they do whatever seems to attack the foundations.

There is a large class, with whom we must sympathize and whose feelings we must spare, if possible, to whom peace, even at the price of truth, is most precious.

It sometimes seems as though truth were like oxygen needing admixture of less vital substances before man can endure it.

Most of mankind are not unwilling to receive a truth provided it does not disarrange their mental storehouse. Like Septimius Severus, the emperor, who placed a statue of Jesus among his gods, so they will introduce a truth on condition that it will accommodate itself to their errors.

Superstitions are like superstructures, one feels safer in them, somehow, than when on the solid rock. And, if they must go, he prefers, much as a man standing on a thirty foot snowdrift prefers, that they melt gradually, that the fall be not too sudden.

But though we must deal as tenderly as possible with what is unreasonable, we must recognize it, and, so far as can be, remove it from our religious persuasions.

There are those to whom authority is supremely acceptable, who prefer mental passivity to activity, and soul-surrender to self-assertion. There are those who greatly prefer the exquisite pleasure of the peace which comes with submission, to the delight and satisfaction which the intellectual explorer finds in the search after and acquisition of truth. In those of whom we speak, reason and conscience are below the imagination and the feelings in effective influence.

The feeling of dependence is mighty, if not almighty, in religion. That which is satisfactory comes to be fact; or, as Cardinal Newman taught, subjective certitude is the test of objective truth.

Superstition is unrecognizable because superstition is perceived by the mind and the mind is quieted with the mere feeling of utility. Thus it happens that just where, theoretically, we might expect caution and scrutiny, that is, in religion, there is the abandonment of the faculty which has created science and filled the world with knowledge. It is in religion, in what concerns the spiritual life that man displays his greatest helplessness and surrenders most readily and even thankfully to what speaks with authority, distrustful of self and trustful of what makes great claims.

Because the issue involved is so eternally important man hesitates to use his reason. Thus, where most of all man should use the " light that is within him," he casts it away and follows, sometimes with infatuated blindness, what glares most vividly over the path of life.

The reply that Manning, before he had passed into the Catholic church, made to Gladstone was most significant. Gladstone asked him what there could be in common among so many of different minds and dispositions which induced them to go into the Catholic church. Manning's answer was slow and deliberate: "Their common bond is their want of truth" (Morley's "Gladstone," I, p. 317).

There is probably no intentional antagonism but only an unconscious indifference to truth. This indifference to truth is most noticeable in the Roman Catholic church, and is an inheritance from ancient Rome. Rome, in general, acted first and thought afterwards. So the Roman church distilled her Christian theory out of her Christian institutions. Neither ancient nor modern Rome has had any strong love for truth as truth. As Pilate said indifferently, what is truth?

The definition of divine truth coming nearest to the catholic conception, as formed by the Roman church, would be "that body of theoretic assumptions which would be needed to justify, on intellectual grounds, all those institutions, special and general, by which practically she had been enabled to win hearts and guide nations" (R. H. Hutton).

Hutton uses as example Newman's treatment of the legend of the assumption of the Virgin Mary. "However we feel," Dr. Newman says, after narrating the

beautiful tradition, " towards the details of this history
(*nor is there anything in it which will be difficult or
unwelcome to piety*) so much cannot be doubted that,
as is befitting, she is body and soul in heaven and that
we have to celebrate not only her death, but her
assumption." So easily are tremendous facts settled
by the eager and willing spirit without evidence!

The natural catholic is not accustomed to ask for,
nor wait for, nor to be affected by, evidence. What
shall be believed is determined on the ground of its
seeming utility, its accord with the sentiments of the
human heart. What is demanded is, not evidence of
validity, but evidence of efficacy. Ecclesiasticism is
the religion of utility, rather than of truth, as even Mr.
Gladstone illustrates, in his later transition.

Brunetierre, the distinguished French author, recently
converted to the catholic faith, when asked what he
believed, could say, without probably intending to
despise the majesty of truth, " Go to Rome and
inquire." It is this which makes it possible for a
Newman and a Kenrick to argue that the infallibility
of the pope is to-day false, and to-morrow accept on
authority that it is God's own truth.

Therefore, there are those who come to this question
of The Church with an inclination which may be said
to determine beforehand their formal decision. There
can be no conception of The Church so agreeable as
that it is an institution to which they can intrust their
immortal interests without a second thought, with no
qualm of anxiety. They desire peace. Why should
not The Church be such an institution as to give it?

To such, then, the priest with his absolution, the priest with his sacrifice, the priest with his intercession and his extreme unction, is most welcome. To such, the belief that a church is infallible, that its bishops are the treasurers of truth, is a belief too precious to be closely scrutinized. The transition from the agitation of the sea of searchings, of uncertainties, of variations, to the calm haven where every thought is stilled by a voice that says, " peace! be still," is all that is desired. There are those who would eat of the lotus, that they may enjoy blissful repose.

Thus we can see how acceptable to many must have been and still is the conception of The Church as an *organization* such that by belonging to it man can secure his salvation.

For the completion of this confidence it was necessary that the catholic church should be regarded as an organization to which Jesus Christ gave all the means of salvation. Therefore this church, as an organization, is the ark of salvation, according to the full-grown catholic conception. Priests can, through baptism, produce regeneration. They can sacrifice the body of Christ in reality. They can transform bread and wine into His very body and blood. They can forgive sin and remit its penalties. They can intercede successfully for the souls in purgatory.

To the catholic, the claim of the bishop to be the channel through whom all this power comes to the priest is satisfactory and therefore true. To the bishop he gladly concedes the knowledge of true doctrine and the ability to confer grace and the Holy Spirit, to the priest in ordination, to the layman in confirmation.

When this concept becomes a reality, as it does especially in the Roman and Greek (Orthodox) Catholic churches, when we see this concept so gorgeously apparelled, as in these churches, so munificently supplied with a wealth of suggestive ritual, so grand in growth, we do not wonder that those who are naturally catholic, naturally inclined to trust to visible agencies, naturally disposed to yield to outward authority, are convinced that in some catholic church The True Church is realized.

This disposition, of which we have been speaking, will have no other church than one which can save them. "There is remission of sins and eternal life through the Church." "There is no salvation out of the Church." "He cannot have God as his Father who has not the Church as his Mother." Quoting such sentences from Cyprian, the great African ecclesiastic, Bishop Gore, of the Anglican church, says: "Communion with God depended on communion with the Church"; and, further, "Jesus Christ instituted the Church as a means of belonging to Him."

There are those to whom God has given a different disposition. In them the right to think and the duty to reason is supreme and imperative, compelling them to find peace, not in authority, not in imposing magnificence and power, not in ritual which soothes the feelings (and too often stupefies the mind), but, if found at all, only after the sea of opinions has been crossed, whose haven lies not this side but the other side of the ocean of errors.

These cannot, without what seems to them moral and mental suicide, surrender their independence, not so much because it is a right as because it is a duty. To them it is a necessity to examine what presents itself in the realm of religion with the same scrutiny as that which presents itself in the realm of science. They cannot conceive that what is true in science can be false in religion, or what is false in religion can be true in science. They can recognize not two but only one world of human thought, and the same methods must apply in ascertaining that which man shall believe throughout the whole universe of the mind. Hence, by an inexorable necessity, which may involve anxiety and unrest, they must search and see what comes out of Nazareth. These must prefer to hear Christ Himself, rather than His vicar; the Apostles, rather than their successors: they must believe that the Spirit of God is as really in themselves as individuals, as it may be in ecclesiastical assemblies.

To such indeed the Jerusalem above is a mother and the Jerusalem on earth but the earthy shadow. They do not understand that Paul teaches " salvation through the Church." Not union with a church, as Gore says, brings one to Christ, but union with Christ brings one to the Church. He is a Christian, as Paul said of a Jew, not, who is one outwardly; but, who is one inwardly (Rom. 2 : 27).

To those who do not feel the need of institutional-ism, The Church is the fellowship of believers, the communion of saints, the household of faith. The Christian naturally belongs to this fellowship for the culture and exercise of his Christian character. The Christian does not join a church in order to gain salvation; he simply associates himself with those who, like himself, are Christians by reason of their faith, their hope, their love (Acts 2: 47). While not seeking salvation through a church, yet the evangelical has abundant reasons for being in Christian fellowship. He cannot thrive alone. It is a question whether he can live alone. There are blessings which God gives to Christians associated together, collectively, that is to a church, which He does not, cannot give, to separate individuals. The first concern is to belong to Jesus Christ; the second concern is to be in communion with others who "have like precious faith."

VI

THE CHURCH OF THE NEW TESTAMENT

The meaning and use of Ecclesia.
How related to synagogos.
The various uses.
The actual meaning :   Christians as a unity.
Few times in which Church is used in its universal sense.
Christ's use of the word kahala.
The house of God.
The second sense: a local body of Christians.
The plural use.
"One " in Christ, not "one" in Galatia.
A church manifests The Church.
McGiffert on The Church and its manifestations.
The church at Ephesus is The Church of God.
The correct use of visible and invisible.
"The faithful in Christ Jesus."
The Christian is the unit of The Church.
The names for "Church members."
The flock and the folds.
"By their fruits ye shall know them."
The opinion of churchmen.
Definitions of The Church.

VI

THE CHURCH OF THE NEW TESTAMENT

WHETHER the evangelic or the catholic concept of The Church is correct, is to be decided by an examination of the actual, existing Church, and not by the study of some imaginary or ought-to-be Church.

We must first ascertain what and where the reality is which we name Church.

To what is this name Church given, as an historical fact.

This must be answered by a study of the use of the word " ecclesia."

" Ecclesia " occurs one hundred and fourteen times in the New Testament. The translation of " ecclesia" by the word " church " is subject to regrets. To have preserved the untranslated word would, probably, have conduced to the maintenance of its original meaning. The better English word is congregation. The word, church, was not used in Matt. 16: 18 until King James' version. (See Hort.)

As it is, the word " church " has come to signify, in the common understanding, what ecclesia did not mean. The word, associated with the adjective catholic has become, we may say, adjectivized.

How easily a word may change its meaning and depart from its original significance is a common fact of language. It is exceedingly difficult to escape from the present meaning of any word to its past or original meaning. For illustration, the word cathedral is now invariably used for a bishop's church, while originally the word referred to nothing else than a chair or stool. But, since the bishop sat in a particular chair, every cathedral became a bishop's seat, and because the seat was in a church, that church edifice became a cathedral.

The word " church," as in current use, misleads from the meaning of Christ's words. Hort rejects the word, saying, " the word ' church' carries with it associations and doctrines derived from later times."

Luther rejected the word " kirche " as " blind and unclear," and substituted for it the word " gemeinde."

Probably Jesus used an Aramaic form of *kahal*. This word might have been translated by either "synagogos " or "ecclesia." The word "synagogos " echoes in Heb. 10:25. It occurs in James 2:2; and Rev. 2:9, and 3:9. Epiphanius says that the Jews " call their ecclesia synagogue and not ecclesia." (See also Heb. 2:12 and Ps. 22:23 LXX.)

The oldest monument of a Christian building is that built by the Marcionites, and is called a synagogue.

The choice of the word "ecclesia" was made for several reasons. The word " synagogue " was pre-empted by the Jews for their assemblies, and hence was not so free for usage among Christians. The word "ecclesia," as Cremer and Hatch and other students inform us, was the name common in the Greek world for the assembly of free citizens called together by a herald and therefore most appropriate to name the Christians whom Christ called together.   Further, ecclesia was the common word used in translating kahal into Greek.   The Christians were the new kahal or congregation of God, the true Israel.

To ascertain what this word ecclesia names we need not go beyond the Septuagint and the New Testament.   Indeed, New Testament usage must be decisive.   It is ample.

The studies of such men as Sohm and Hatch and Hort and Lindsay and Bannerman and many others make it unnecessary to examine this usage afresh. Lindsay bases his classification of usage on Hort. Hort finds eleven shades of meaning.   Lindsay uses a fourfold classification.   Bannerman reduces all to three groups.   Two usages suffice for our classification.

The word, church, as used in the singular and in the plural in the New Testament makes evident that The Church is, in the universal and ideal sense, nothing other than the total number of disciples or Christians, who are also the heirs to God's salvation.   In its secondary sense, both in the singular and in the plural, it designates a particular company, larger or smaller, of God's children who come together in the fellowship of Christian faith, hope and love.   In this latter sense *a church and the churches are manifestations of the One True Church.*

" Ecclesia" always names an assemblage of people. It is so used of the mob in the circus at Ephesus (Acts 19 : 32, 39, 41).   Calvin interpets ecclesia in Matt. 18 : 17 as the synagogue of the Jews.   Acts 7 : 38

refers to the people of God, Israel in the wilderness. Otherwise, ecclesia in the New Testament names Christians as these are regarded as one body in Christ Jesus, or any number of Christians, in some particular locality, either thought of as an associated body, or as met together for worship.

The cases where ecclesia names the mere assemblage for worship are few, hardly requiring separate classification: in 1 Cor. 11 : 18, " When ye are come in church," " en ecclesia " is adverbial for, " when ye are come together as a church for worship," so also in 1 Cor. 14 : 19, " I would rather speak five words intelligently in the church," is " en ecclesia " ; and in 1 Cor. 14 : 4 " edifies the church." The sense is : the temporary meeting together of Christians.

For understanding, it is not necessary to find more than two usages of the word ecclesia in the New Testament, whether singular or plural; namely, where the word names the body of Christians conceived as a totality, a whole; and where it names the Christians of a particular locality, be it large or small.

That is, *ecclesia always names either all Christians, or some Christians as one in Christ Jesus, one in faith, hope and love.* That Christians should not form a church is never suggested as a possibility. *Where Christians are, there a church is of necessity,* and there also The Church is manifest. *Christians of necessity constitute a church and The Church.* These two facts are of great significance.

The Church is the total number of those " who are in Christ Jesus " (1 Thess. 2 : 14), *The Church* is manifest in *a church*, which is a body or association of Christians in a locality, be it country, city or house.

The cases in which The Whole Church is spoken of are few and should be noted.

In Acts 5 : 11, 8 : 1, 8 : 3, reference is not made to The Universal Church, but only to that portion of the body of Christians which was in Judea. The same is true all through the book of Acts (as in Acts 15 : 3, 4) ; not even is Acts 20 : 28, "to feed the Church of God" an exception, but here we have an illustration of the second usage, in which the local church is regarded as a manifestation of the Church of God, as is said, "the Church of God which is at Corinth" (1 Cor. 1 : 2; 2 Cor. 1 : 1).

The whole, universal Church, as distinct from its manifestation (second sense) in a church, is spoken of only in the letters to the Ephesians (eight times); to the Colossians (twice) and in 1 Tim. 3 : 15. Heb. 2 : 12 and Heb. 12 : 23 probably should be included. In these passages, ecclesia names the body, the total number of the new humanity redeemed in Christ the Head. This is the universal, ideal sense of The Church, corresponding to the "Israel of God" of the Old Testament.

When Christ says, "On this rock I will build My Church" (we assume these words to be genuine although Reville and others assign fair reasons for disputing them), He refers to the structure of human souls which He proposed building upon God, the everlasting foundation. This Church is not regarded as an organized society, as we shall see, but all the faithful

who constitute Christ's Church are to be built into the
Kingdom of God. Dr. Briggs' suggestion is (" Messiah of the Gospels," p. 191), that Jesus meant by
" Kahala " here, " I will build My Kingdom," and that
Kingdom and church are identified in this passage.
The idea is true enough that what Jesus calls His
Kahala or ecclesia is nothing else than the constituent
members of the Kingdom of. God who are such because they accept Him as Christ. " *My Church*"
here means the " *habitation of God, through the spirit*"
which He was building. Jesus will build again God's
tabernacle. The " house of God," both that called
Israel and this new house into which the old elements
are to be brought, are His work. Jesus regards the
true Israel as henceforth His, He has come to claim
them and will save them, He is God's shepherd, the
true shepherd of the sheep. He will build again
God's tabernacle. This figure of a building is ampli-
fied in Hebrews 3 : 1–6. " Consider Christ Jesus.
. . . This man was counted worthy of more glory
than Moses, inasmuch as he who hath builded the
house hath more honour than the house. He that
hath built all things is God. Moses was faithful as a
servant ; but Christ as a son over His own house ;
whose house are we."

Thus *The Church*, the tabernacle, the temple, the
house which Jesus Christ is building, *is the one house
of God in which Moses was a servant.* (See also Ps.
74 : 2 and Acts 20 : 28.)

The second sense in which church is used, is to
name *any local body of Christians*, who *because* they

are, and *so far* as they are, Christians are one body. That this is true is immediately apparent. Out of the one hundred and ten times that the word ecclesia (singular and plural) is used concerning Christians, excepting ten (see Lindsay), the word does not name the one whole church but a local society.

There are the *churches* of God (1 Thess. 2 : 14; 1 Cor. 11 : 16). There is not one church in Asia, but many (1 Cor. 16 : 19). Not one in Rome, but more (Rom. 16 : 16). There are many Gentile churches (Rom. 16 : 4). In Galatia the number is plural (Gal. 1 : 2). Even in Judea there are " churches " (Gal. 1 : 22), which are " in Christ." ·These are distinct, or the plural would not be used. The churches are *one in God*, in Christ, *not one in Galatia*, as an organization. " The churches of Judea have rest." There is a church in the house (meeting in the house) of Philemon, Each of the cities of Asia has a church. Paul is burdened with the care of the churches. Yet, each of these churches may be called The Church of God. Indeed, if not representing The Church of God, it is not a church of God. But, it must be instantly added, there is never in the apostolic usage the slightest notion that a church is the total of The Church, but simply a manifestation of The Church.

We might regard this as a third sense : when a church is distinctly made representative of the whole Church, as " The Church of God which is at Corinth," " I persecuted The Church of God." But, as there cannot be a church which is not a manifestation of The Church, this is not a third sense. The thought is ex-

ceeding simple; Christians compose The Church in
the large sense; therefore, a company of Christians
anywhere can be called by this name, indifferently, a
church or a manifestation of The Church of God, in
one case " churches of Christ " (Rom. 16 : 16).

The reason why a local company of Christians is
called " a church," or " the church," or " the church of
God," is, as already said, because it is a manifestation of
the one Church. As McGiffert says, " If we would understand it, we must remember that the universal church
did not grow out of the local congregations, but that
they grew out of it; that they believed themselves to
be simply manifestations of the Kingdom of God"
(" Apostolic Age," p. 646). " The church in the city
or in the house, is simply a local manifestation of the
Church of God; there is in reality only one Church,
as there is only one body of Christ." " It was a long
time before the conception of the one Church of God
found expression in organization " (*Ib.*, p. 638). Organizations never covered, only *claimed* to cover, the
whole fact, as there continued to be churches which
were never catholic, after the rise of catholicism.

But, because these independent churches were made
up of Christians, men of faith and hope and love in
Christ, however scattered, however different in government, or no government, however divergent in degree
of holiness and purity of doctrine, so far as Christian
these churches were all regarded as representing The
One Church of God, which was purchased with the
blood of Jesus Christ.

The churches, as associations of Christians, represent

The Church.   There is no question that Paul calls
these assemblies, whether in a province, in a city, or
in a house, churches, even The Church, as manifest-
ing The One Church of God.

The church of Ephesus is called The Church of God,
not as being the whole Church, but as having in itself;
and for itself all that God can give and be to the whole
Church.   He " purchased it."   It belongs to Him.

Paul addresses the Thessalonian believers as " The
church that is in God and in Jesus Christ."   This fact
united this church to all other churches similarly in
God, in Christ.   But the union did not interfere with
independence.

It would have been impossible to have called these
collections of Christians at Antioch, at Ephesus, at
Jerusalem, a or the church unless they represented the
whole Church of God in that locality.

The Church as manifest in the churches is referred
to in Acts 20 : 28, " Feed the Church of God over
which God has made you overseers," namely, so much
of The Church of God which is at Ephesus.   So the
Corinthians constitute The Church of God at Corinth
(1 Cor. 1 : 2; 2 Cor. 1 : 1; 1 Cor. 11 : 22).

When Paul " persecuted the Church of God," it was
this Church *as manifest* in Judea.

Objection must be made to the term " invisible " as
applied to The Church.   *The Church is never totally
visible nor totally invisible* in the absolute and ideal
sense; as a universal Church, The Church is not visible, in its totality.   But, on the other hand, The
Church is and always must be visible because every

Christian community, indeed, every Christian, is a
manifestation of that Church. That is, *The Church is
never invisible.* The Churches manifest The Church.
Christ, as the Head of The Church, is personally invisible, yet Christ is manifest and visible in Christians;
so The Church is visible in the churches, and in no
other way.

It is sometimes assumed by catholics that the visibility of The Church depends upon its organization in
one form. But, a mob is as visible as the most thoroughly organized society. A people is as visible as a
nation. As Charles Hodge says (" Church Polity,"
p. 65), " The Church is no more invisible than believers are." Because, believers constitute The Church,
the separate churches manifest The Church.

.   The common notion which underlies both these
uses of the word ecclesia is that of disciple or Christian, the " faithful in Christ Jesus " constitute The
Church and a church. Paul in writing to Rome does
not use ecclesia, but addresses his letter to " all that
are called to be saints, beloved of God." This phrase
is equivalent to " Church." " Church" names in the
New Testament, Christians, saints, believers, the faithful and hopeful ones in Christ, regarded as a unity
whether in the sense of a totality or some local manifestation of that totality.

Hort says, The Church is " made up of all the *members* of the many ecclesiæ." Yet, though this nearly
covers the truth, the objection to it is, that it seems to
make *The Church* dependent on *the churches,* whereas
the reverse is true. *The churches are made from the*

members of The Church. But Hort's distinction is not open to Moberly's objection that it is " hardly intelligible " to say that The Church is made up of the members of the ecclesiæ and not made up of the many ecclesiæ. The distinction is plain enough. Despite its name, the " United States," as the Civil War decided, is not made up of states, but of citizens under state government. It is, as the Preamble to the Constitution says: " We, *the people* of the United States, in order to form a more perfect union." All the churches in Christendom added together as pieces of a dissected map do not make *The* Church. But as Paul says: " We, being many members in one body." A local church—and that may mean a national church —is but a needful, almost necessary, convenience for the benefit of the local Christians of the nation. The local church is not the unit in Christ's body, but the individual Christian. Therefore there might be church union without Christian union. The Anglican church furnishes abundant illustration of that, as indeed all churches do, to a greater or less extent.

Paul's conception of the ideal, which is also the real Church, is not that which was later understood as " catholic." There is no indication that Paul strove after any other unity than that which was the unity of faith and hope and love.

The only reason why the name, church, can be given to any one of many local communities of churches is because *The Church* is *wherever Christians are in the unity of faith, hope and love,* be they few or many. Christians, the children of the Word, are the

units which constituted the local churches. The Word
of God gives the Church its life.

Confirming our definition of The Church are the
names used to designate those who compose the
churches: (Phil. 1: 1; Eph. 1: 1; Col. 1: 2; Rom.
1: 7; 1 Cor. 1: 2; 1 Cor. 6: 11; 1 Thess. 1: 1; 2: 14).

The present custom of calling Christians "churchmen" or "church members" has no warrant in primitive custom, and has become a vicious custom.

The earliest name for Christians was disciples.
From this we learn that the first church was of the
nature of a school, such as the Greek teachers, Plato or
Zeno formed. A school is a visible body but it, or-
dinarily, is not an organized body except as it is under
a master. The only Master, Jesus distinctly says, is to
be Himself (Matt. 23: 8, 10). And Paul forbids the
Christians at Corinth calling themselves followers of any
apostle. The transgression of this law in both catholic
and protestant churches has wrought great evil.

The Church is not named, but is meant, when it is
said that "the Lord added together those that were
being saved" (Acts 2: 47). Here the composition
of The Church is, those either saved or in process of
salvation, as one may prefer to translate it. A designation that occurs frequently in Acts (9: 2; 22: 4;
24: 14) as naming The Church is "those of the
Way"; that is, those of the persuasion, conviction,
conduct which had Jesus Christ as its author and per-
fector.

In the Epistles, the addresses tell us that the
churches are made up "of saints"; that is, those

sanctified, set apart, as belonging to God; the
"called." "To all that are in Rome, called to be
saints" (Rom. 1: 7). "To the church of God at
Corinth, even them that are sanctified in Christ
Jesus, called to be saints. With all that call upon the
name of our Lord Jesus in every place" (1 Cor 1 : 2).
Here we have the description of the *One True Holy
Catholic Apostolic Church ;* it is all those who in every
place call upon the name of, that is, believe in Jesus as
Lord.

The same is said in 2 Cor. 1: 1, " Unto the church
at Corinth, with all the saints that are in the whole
of Achaia." Here is the old Greek church, *i. e.,* all
the saints in Greece. There are numerous churches or
congregations in Galatia (1 : 2). These churches are
manifestly in a dangerous condition, near to a fall
from grace. How can these be churches if they, as at
Corinth, contain those as members who are " be-
witched " or evil doers? Because, the local church,
though it be a manifestation of The Church of God
(1 Cor. 1 : 2) yet is an *imperfect* manifestation. That
a perfect thing may have an imperfect manifestation
need not surprise us, because in coming to manifestation it takes on elements which may not be perfectly
assimilated or even have spiritual affinity. Thus a
peace society, like the Quakers, cannot be judged by
some local society of Friends in which are advocates
of war. These do not *belong* to the society as a matter of fact; they merely *adhere* to it in a superficial
way. A ship may enter into a harbour with its hull
covered with barnacles, but no one would say the

barnacles belonged to the ship. Traitors may seem to belong to an army in which they are enrolled, but they do not. Ananias and Sapphira did not *belong* to The Church of God at Jerusalem, though they were recognized, until the end came, as members in good standing of the Jerusalem Church. In this sense, then, The Church has *apparently belonging to it those who are not of it.* Thus a Church, as some of those in Asia, might have so many members who were not saints, that ultimately it might lose its life as a heap of cinders may extinguish a fire. *The Church does not die,* because the Word of God is quick and powerful, imperishable, and always regenerating some, somewhere. An Elijah is not the only survivor of the true religion.

The letters to the Ephesians and Colossians and Philippians are to the saints or the faithful brethren in Christ. These constitute the substance of God's Church. The Church of God at Thessalonica consists of those who are " brethren," " those who have turned from the idols unto the living God and to wait for His Son from heaven."

Here (1 : 3) we have the threefold characteristics of the Christian and therefore of The Church set forth with exactness ; " your work of faith ; your labour of love; your patience of hope." *These three elements constitute the Churchship of the Thessalonians and of all churches, and characterize The Church of God.*

The phrase in 2 Thess., " The church of the Thessalonians in God," is singular but it is significant. The ecclesia or collected Christians of Thessalonica are

" in God." In this letter also the elements of faith anc
hope and love constantly appear.

As in other epistles, The Church is the " household o
faith," the fellowship of the saints, so in 1 Tim. (3 : 15
the Church of God is called the house of God ; and s〔
in Heb. (3 : 6), " whose house are we," and in 2 Cor
(6 : 16), the church is a temple of God.

Each individual is a miniature of the one Church o
Temple, himself the body of Christ. Paul make〔
Christ, or God, head of a threefold body ; the singl〔
man (1 Cor. 11 : 3), the many in a single church (2 Cor
11 ; 2), and of the totality (Eph. 4).

In other words, all these name The Church as being
the company of those who as God's children, as living
stones, are dwelt in by God and His Spirit. But
as the passage in Hebrews says, this being in God'〔
House is conditional on the holding fast the confidenc〔
and the rejoicing of their hope firm unto the end.

" First Peter " is sent to the " sojourners of the Dis
persion," the elect " according to the foreknowledge o
God, in sanctification of the spirit, unto obedience an〔
sprinkling of the blood of Jesus Christ" (1 : 1), and
" 2 Peter" is sent to such as have " like preciou〔
faith" (1 : 1). In 1 John, The Church is evidentl〕
those who hold fellowship with the Father and th〔
Son, and who are constantly cleansed by the blood o
Jesus Christ.

The True Church is the whole flock of Jesus Chris〔
Any organized church with bounds of inclusion an
exclusion *is not the flock, but a fold* of larger or sma〔
dimension.

Therefore, no single church can be *The* Church. There is to be one shepherd and one flock (John 10 : 16).

The identification of flock and fold, as in the " catholic" churches, has been a frightful heresy.

The Church is the " church of the first-born," the new born. It is the new, the true, humanity (Eph. 1 : 10; Col. 1 : 20).

The Church, we conclude, is *visible* wherever any Christians are living in the one faith, hope and love. It is *one*, beneath all superficial differences, in the unity of the Spirit. It is *holy*, in the being inwardly called by the Spirit to sanctification. It is *catholic*, in that it includes all believers. It is *apostolic*, or better, Christian, having only Christ as its founder, as its builder, as its teacher, through His Spirit.

As the right to the name Christian cannot be finally determined by human perception, so is the determination of the right of a church to that name beyond the reach of man's perception. Yet the same general rule applies to both; by their fruits ye shall know them.

In the criticism which the Spirit makes of the churches of Asia there is the repetition of the words : I know thy works.

The doctrine taught is also a determinative factor.

There is complete silence as to any connection with the "catholic" church as basis of judgment. What saves the church at Sardis is that " thou hast a few names even in Sardis which have not defiled their garments and they shall walk with me in white, for they are worthy."

The idea or concept of The Church, as the embodiment of the Spirit of God, or the Spirit of Christ, is clearly set forth in the letter to the Ephesians. The Church is regarded as already in existence even before the coming of Jesus. There were those who " hoped beforehand in Christ" (1 : 12). (See Ellicott, Com. s. l.) That is, the men of hope, such as Paul was himself before his conversion, are regarded as constituent elements of The Church. In this same sense, Christ is said to be "given to The Church" (1: 22), so that The Church becomes His body. The newly converted Gentiles are regarded as being brought into The Church, the " Commonwealth of Israel" (2 : 11), through their faith in Christ. Thus one body is formed of the old and the new and reconciled to God. These "aliens" are received into The Church, are made " fellow citizens with the saints and of the household of God" (2: 19), " for a habitation of God in the Spirit" (2: 22). This constant use of the word "fellow" tells us that the writer regards The Church as having existed in the earlier dispensation. These "strangers," as the Jews regarded them, are to be welcomed to that old household to which God had been a Father and *to which* He sent His Son. The contrast which is implied in the reiterated use of "Gentile" is not Christian, but Jew. So that Paul here clearly teaches that the faithful Jews already constituted The Church which is henceforth to include both Jew and Gentile and all who are men of faith and hope and love. " To make all men see what is the dispensation of the mystery—to the intent that

through The Church the manifold wisdom of God
might be made known " (Eph. 2 : 10).

This Church is the " Pleroma "; it is that which
Christ fills (Eph. 1 : 23). This is the concept of The
Church : The Pleroma of the Spirit. There is " one
body" (Eph. 4 : 4). " The whole community of Chris-
tians," says Ellicott (s. l.), " is the mystical body of
Christ."

That there is any other " head " than Christ, is
excluded. It is evident that all those pertain to this
body who have Christ as their head. All those who
have this " One Lord, one faith, one baptism," *constitute* The Church. That there is any external band
or bond, Paul nowhere hints. The unity is that of
" lowliness, meekness, longsuffering, forbearing one
another in love." To enable this Church to grow up
perfectly there are apostles, prophets, evangelists, pastors and teachers (Eph. 4 : 11), who *serve it*, but do
not constitute it. These make " increase of the body
unto the building up of itself in love."

To conclude, these and other New Testament teachings justify the conception of The Church as the whole
body of those who *are* one body because there lives
in all the parts one Spirit. No lesser definition of
The Church is, scripturally, possible than that this
word names the complete company, however scattered
on earth, of those who have affinity with God. The
" saints " constitute The Church. And by " saints "
Paul unmistakably means those who have working in
them the Spirit of God, which is the Spirit of Christ.

Schleiermacher is therefore justified in regarding the

triumphant Church as the sum of all the efforts of the Spirit.

So also to Ritschl, as to Luther, and Calvin, and Huss, before him, The Church is the communion of the saints which can never have the visibility of an institution.

This New Testament concept of The Church prevailed until the dominance of catholicism.

So Tertullian says: "The very Church itself is the Spirit Himself" (Modesty, 21). And again: "Every number of persons who may be combined together into this faith is accounted a church."

Earlier, Origen says: "The Holy Scriptures declare the body of Christ to be the whole Church of God, and the members of this body to consist of those who are believers" (Ag. Cel., 48).

That which constitutes The Church, constitutes a church according to Origen: "In every association of Christians are the angels and the power of Christ and the spirits of all believers." The whole Church is present, spiritually; in a church, it is representatively there. And, as Tertullian loved to emphasize, where three are, there is Christ and there is a church.

To conclude, the New Testament teaches that "The Church" never should mean anything other than the body of Christ, which has as its component parts those called in the New Testament faithful, or saints, or the hopeful in God.

And every separate company of such is a church.

Concerning organization or government or form of worship, the New Testament is singularly reticent.

In accord with this opinion, from among many we may cite a few writers.

Augustine says: " The whole Church is made up of all the faithful, because the faithful are members of Christ; these may be separated in sight but are bound in love."

Chrysostom calls The Church " the multitude of believers." Among later writers we may cite Bishop Jewell: " The church is the ' fellow citizens with the saints ' . . . such a church are they who in any place of the world truly fear the Lord and call upon His name."

Hatch says The Church is " the whole congregation of Christian people dispersed throughout the world."

Hort says, The Church is " the community of Christians as a whole, all in whom Christ dwells as units are stones of the Eternal Tabernacle; when each stone is perfect the temple is complete."

Canon Bruce (" Apostolic Order," p. 123), quotes from John Hooper, Bishop and Martyr, A. D. 1551: " The Church of God is not by God's word taken for the multitude of bishops, priests, and such others; but it is the company of all men hearing God's Word and obeying the same, lest any man should be seduced, believing himself to be bound to any ordinary succession of bishops and priests, but only to the Word of God and the right use of the Sacraments."

In the office of the Holy Communion in the English Book of Prayer, The Church is " the mystical body of Thy son, *which is the blessed company of all faithful people.*

VII

CHRIST AND THE CHURCH

Did The Church originate with Jesus?
Paul's teaching.
"Church of Jesus Christ" an unknown phrase in New Testament.
God's covenant one and everlasting.
Jeremiah and the covenant.
Jesus and the New Covenant.
The torah a mere episode.
Two testaments, but one Bible.
The relation of Jesus to The Church.
The Church never defunct.
Faith, hope, love the constituting elements.
The new Israel is the true old Israel.
"My Church."
The disciples, this Church, has no organization.
How the Christian Church came into separate being.
The rejection of Jesus and His disciples.
The true Israelite.

VII

CHRIST AND THE CHURCH

CANON, now Bishop, Gore, makes a statement which is of fundamental importance to the catholic position, but which is based on a misunderstanding of the facts. He says: " Jesus founded a visible society or church to be the organ of His spirit, the depository of His truth, the sphere of His redemptive grace " (" Christian Ministry," p. 337). This sentence, seemingly true, must be examined, that the fallacy may be evident.

If it were true, it would go far to establish the catholic position. If Jesus Christ began or organized a set, fixed, formal association, that association should be maintained in its original form. Facts do not sustain this catholic claim.

The Church of God was not created nor even re-created by Jesus Christ. It is here, at the very outset, that the catholic concept of The Church misses verification.

The Church of God—and there is no other true Church—*existed before Jesus Christ came among men*. There is no suggestion in the New Testament that The Church was called into being by Jesus Christ. The familiar " high " or catholic church sentence, " Christ came on earth to establish The Church," is without New Testament warrant. He came to redeem God's People, The Church.

The Apostle Paul is, especially, authority for the antiquity of The Church. For him, the idea or concept of The Church is covered by the word, "covenant." He constantly insists that the covenant, which really chartered The Church, was older than Moses by four hundred years. Likewise, the author of Hebrews dates the priesthood of Christ, typically, from Melchizedek, the contemporary of Abraham. *The Church of God was already in existence* when Jesus came to minister unto it. Paul says, " Jesus Christ was a minister of the circumcision for the truth of God to confirm the promises made unto the fathers" (Rom. 15 : 8). This fundamental fact which appears luminously not only in Paul's letters but also in the gospel of Christ's life and words, is overlooked and ignored by the " catholic" who assumes that Jesus Christ created The Church. Charles Hodge correctly says, " When Christ came The Church remained " (" Church Polity," p. 67).

Before Christ came there was a " society, the home of grace and truth," to use favourite phrases of Bishop Gore, there was a " home of the new covenant of salvation." Jesus recognized Israel as such a home. It was the Israel of God Jesus came to save. And, the gospel of Jesus was primarily to arouse all true Israelites to a life of faith and hope, in view of the certain advent of the Kingdom of God. The Kahala, Ecclesia, congregation, was the company of the faithful who responded to His call. The covenant was not " new " in the sense of " another." It is an error to suppose that, even though grace and truth find their fullest revela-

tion in Jesus Christ that these are new with Him
This is as wrong as supposing that all law ende
with Moses and that Christ was not law as well a
grace and truth.

The old dispensation ran into the new one as earl
spring into summer fullness and autumnal harvest
One might, with as much justification say that th
summer originated with the August sun.

It is a most significant fact that the phrase, " *Th
Church of Jesus Christ,*" *is never used in the Nei
Testament,* while the phrase " The Church of God " i
used a number of times.   The " Churches of Christ
are twice spoken of (Rom. 16: 16; 1 Cor. 11: 16
just as the " churches of God " are mentioned (1 Thes:
2 : 14) but never the Church of Christ.   *This fact ha
never been duly considered.*

The relation which Jesus sustained to The Churc
is not that of creator nor originator.   Paul is clear o
this point. (See Eph. 5: 23–32.)   The figures t
designate the relation of Jesus to The Church exclud
the idea of founder.   Jesus is the head, the saviou
of The Church.   The Church is His bride.

To understand what The Church was to Jesus w
must understand the idea of the covenant.   Dr. Ho
has called attention to this and he has thereby dor
a good service.   It is quite common to think of th
new covenant as something absolutely new, as thoug
the old covenant was cut off, dead and buried, an
that God created a new covenant people entirely di:
tinct from the old, and a new arrangement or methc
of redemption.   This is a dangerous error.

God has had but one covenant. He has never proposed to man two methods of salvation, the one the law, the other grace; one of works, the other of mercy.

God's covenant is an " everlasting covenant," and it is always with the righteous and there cannot be two ways of becoming righteous, one for yesterday and a new one to-day, one for the day before Jesus was born, or died, and another the day after. God never makes covenant except with the righteous, neither does He make a new covenant in the sense of any alteration of the divine purpose or method.

The way to be righteous is unalterably and everlastingly one. Jesus did not show any new way. It was clearer, plainer, than the way of Moses and Elias, but not different. The path of Jesus is the path Isaiah showed to Irsael, walking with God by faith.

The old revelation may be moonlight, the new sunlight, but the way which these reveal is the same and the covenant of God with those on the way is one and the same.

It is new only as the bud is new, as the blossom is new, as the fruit is new. There is no break in God's plan, no alteration of His purpose. " It shall be well with the righteous," is the everlasting covenant. Grace, mercy and peace are for all those who put their trust in the Lord, hope in His Kingdom, open their hearts to the divine love.

When Jeremiah predicts the new covenant, it is in the same sense that Jesus says: a new commandment. It is that God will write His laws on man's heart, so that what had been outward comes within. *The new covenant is the coming within man of the law, it is no alteration of the divine law.* Man's relation to it is more real, more spiritual. We must not imagine that the prophecy of Jeremiah (32: 37) had no fulfillment until Jesus came:

> "I will bring them again to this place,
> I will cause them to dwell safely
> They shall be my people,
> And I will be their God
> And I will give them one heart and one way
> That they may fear me forever
> For the good of them and their children after them."

Jeremiah is clearly thinking of the covenant of grace which God has with the Israel of the captivity, when He shall "bring again the captivity of Israel" (Jer. 32: 37).

> "At the same time I will be the God of all the families of Israel
> And they shall be my people.
> The people which were left of the sword found grace in the
>   wilderness;
> Even Israel when I went to cause him to rest.
> The Lord hath appeared of old unto me saying,
> Yea, I have loved thee with an everlasting love." (Jer. 31: 1-3.)

The "new" covenant is simply the "old" covenant renewed with those whom God brings back from the Babylonish captivity.

> "He that hath scattered Israel will gather him,
>   And keep him as a shepherd does his flock;
>   For the Lord hath redeemed Jacob,
>   And ransomed him from the hand of the One stronger than he."
>   (Jer. 31: 10, 11.)

It is this ransomed people with whom God renews
His covenant. God has sufficiently afflicted them.
" Like as I have watched over them, to pluck up and
to beat down, to destroy and afflict, so will I watch over
them to build and to plant. Behold the day is come
that I will make a new covenant with the house of
Israel and with the house of Judah, not according to
the covenant that I made with their fathers, on the day
that I took them by the hand to bring them out of the
land of Egypt, which my covenant they brake although I was an husband unto them. But this shall
be the covenant that I will make with the house of
Israel; after those days I will put my law in their inward parts and write it on their hearts, and will be
their God and they shall be my people" (Jer.
31 : 32).

This then is the new covenant, it is that the righteous shall have God's law in their hearts. " I will put
my fear in their hearts, that they shall not depart from
me."

The covenant is renewed because the people are renewed.

What makes the covenant new is not anything new
on God's part except as to what we may call the divine
law of progression from the without to the within.
What is new is the people, who are separated from the
old, as a new branch, as the " root out of the dry
ground." The covenant has so far new objects, in that
it is not with a collective people who are living under
one government and obeying the same outwardly
written laws and customs; but with a people who as

individuals are those of a new heart, the born-again
ones.   So Paul says, " Come out from among them
(the children of Belial) and be ye separate and I will
receive you, and will be a Father unto you and ye
shall be my sons and daughters " (2 Cor. 6: 17).
Nicodemus, Jesus said, should have understood this.
Yet, how many since Nicodemus have misunderstood
the doctrine of the new birth !

All that decayed of the old covenant was its outwardness, the ordinances of divine service (Hebrews
8, 9, 10).   These passed away.   The " new " covenant
has " better " that is, clearer " promises " (Heb.
8 : 6).   *These promises are however not new*, they are
as old as Jeremiah, although the entrance into them
came in fullness only with Jesus Christ and the fuller
gift of the Holy Ghost.

Jesus is " the mediator of the new covenant," because through Him the spirit comes into man's heart.
Through Him man enters, not in a shadowy way but
in a real way, into divine sonship and fellowship. Yet
Paul is at great pains to show that the covenant is one
and always the same, that the covenant of grace was
made with Abraham long before the " law was given
to or by Moses."   There has never been more than
one method of righteousness, Paul teaches.   The law,
that is the Mosaic law (not the moral law), was never
intended as a basis for the divine covenant.   It was a
pedagogue, a slave-tutor, when God's children were, indeed, children and foolish and needed an external law
rather than an internal light.

Paul says, this law did not affect the original

covenant of promises God made with Abraham, with faith as the basis on man's part. God is one and is unalterable. His covenant is everlasting, unchangeable.

Paul says that God never intended that " righteousness " should be by the Mosaic law (Gal. 3: 16). It was, Paul says, a *penal code*, " added because of transgressions." There never was a covenant of law or works succeeded by a covenant of faith. God is one and *faith has ever and always been that which brought man within the covenant.* (See Heb. 11.)

The " Law of Moses " is a mere episode within the everlasting covenant. God has had but one covenant and but one covenant people, those who are true children of Abraham, that is the faithful ones. This covenanted people has existed in all ages and yet comes out into full evidence only in Jesus Christ. " We are all the children of God by faith in Jesus Christ " (Gal. 3: 26) whatsoever one's birth or nationality.

The new covenant therefore is the old covenant just as Jesus said: " A *new* commandment I give unto you which ye have *heard from the beginning.*" It is new in its fullest realization, in its clear revelation. Yet He also calls it " old." It is like the grace of God which though from everlasting finds full manifestation in Jesus Christ. " The grace of God hath appeared " (Titus 2: 11).

Thus there are two testaments but only one Bible. The Gospel is an everlasting Gospel, and, God's people have been from the beginning.

Therefore what is called The Church in the New Testament was not Christ's new creation. It was not a beginning of the true Israel. Jesus recognized Nathaniel as an Israelite, and there were many others. Jesus was the representative of The True Church, not its creator. He was a shepherd of sheep, He was not a maker of sheep. He was come to collect all God's sheep, even those without the fold of ancient Israel (John 10: 16). Jesus was helper, seeker, pastor, saviour. The Church existed elementally before Jesus came. He annexed His ministry to that of John the Baptist, as John connected his to the older prophets. As Stephen says, The Church was "in the wilderness" (Acts 7: 38). Jesus was to "gather into one the children of God that were scattered abroad" (John 11: 52).

The Church of Christ is the true Israel adopted by Him and led forth by Him to redemption and the Kingdom of God. Those who are the true Israel are those who recognize and receive Jesus as their Christ and Redeemer, who having faith and hope and love, make Him their head, whether these be called Jews or Gentiles. (See Rom. 2: 29, and Paul's many statements to this effect.)

We should err if we assumed that the word Kahala (church or congregation) indicated that Jesus was creating a new thing, or causing an organization to arise de novo. It was crystallization and not creation. Jesus did not speak the word of the gospel for the first time. He found a church, He made it His own. He was a builder, not a creator (Matt. 16: 18).

Despite the decay of the ancient house of God there

remained many living stones. Amid the many faith-
less who were nominal, but not actual, children of
Abraham, there were also, how many we cannot tell,
as in the days of Elijah, who had not " bowed the
knee to Baal."   Preceded by His illustrious forerun-
ner, who had summoned all Israel to repent and believe, and who had thus made a beginning of calling
together the elements destined to form the new Israel,
Jesus Himself immediately commenced, as soon as He
heard the call of the Divine Voice, to prepare a people who should inherit the Kingdom of God.

By word and deed He aroused many to the exercise
of faith in His gospel, of hope in the coming kingdom, of love as the full measure of the divine command. Jesus made disciples. His disciples were not
merely those who forsook their ordinary avocation
and gave Him all their time and attention, but all in
whose hearts His word lodged, as good seed producing
the fruit which was itself the beginning of the reign
of God in the human heart. These were the true
Israel, a part of the ancient covenant people. To such
Jesus spoke His beatitudes as promises.

The fact is often overlooked, but it is of great significance, that Jesus recognizes John's work as His
own work, since He takes up his message. This
makes it clear that Jesus regarded the *new Israel* as
nothing else than the *true old Israel*. Every true
child of Abraham was a virtual member of Christ's
Church, every one who believed and obeyed the call
of the gospel of the Kingdom. Therefore we cannot
say that Jesus created The Church. He gives this

name " My Church " to those who believed His message, those who, as Nathaniel, were Israelites indeed,
as Zaccheus, children of Abraham, all who are the
children of God by faith (Gal. 3 : 26).

It would be contrary to fact if we assumed that it
was the primary intention of Jesus to *organize* these
believers into a society distinct from the old Israel,
and to lead them forth as Moses had led Israel out of
Egypt.

Jesus called for no secession.   The Church or new
Israel, as distinct from old Israel, was the result of the
expulsion of the new by the old.   Those who followed
Jesus were to be cast out of the synagogue (John 9 : 34).
Jesus spoke rather with the hope that His word, like
leaven, might leaven the whole mass.   It was *all* Israel
He wanted, " the lost sheep of Israel."   His heart's
desire had been to gather them all under His wing, as
a hen her chickens, but they would not.

It became, however, soon apparent that though He
came unto those who were nominally "His own,"
these received Him not.   But " to as many as received
Him, He gave power and right to be the sons of
God."   The call to all the weary and heavy laden
found, apparently, but few responding.   The people
were too absorbed in their cares to look up.   The
more outwardly religious among them could not com-
prehend a teacher whose words were so different from
the " law " and the traditions.   The seat of Moses was
occupied by pharisees.   And the Sadducees cared for
little else than the enjoyment of the shadow of authority left them by their conquerors.

The rejection of Jesus Christ by Israel as a nation
(not as individuals) caused Him to say that the kingdom would pass from them and be given to others.
This meant, that out of the old Israel officially rejected
there would rise a new Israel, and this new Israel would
carry the gospel to the nations. What God had
threatened to do in the wilderness, make Moses the
head of a new Israel, this He did by Jesus Christ.
*This did not exclude the old as individuals, but as a
secular organization.* Of these individuals God was
forming a new body of which Jesus Christ was the
head. It was the whole company of the new Israel,
the Israel of the new covenant whom the New Testament called Ecclesia, those whom Paul calls the " remnant according to the election of grace " (Rom. 11 : 6).

We call The Church the Christian Church because
the true members of God's Church recognize and accept Jesus as the Christ.

As the Israelite was one faithful to Moses, so the
Christian Church is composed of those making evident
their recognition and acceptance of Jesus as Messiah.

There never was a time when a genuine member of
God's Church would have rejected, except in ignorance,
as Paul did, Jesus as God's Christ.

Such a temporal rejection of Christ, Paul teaches
(Rom. 11), leads to a *temporary* rejection of Israel.
" Blindness in part is happened to Israel, until the
fullness of the Gentiles be come in, and so all Israel
shall be saved." Israel is perpetually the object of
God's love. " As touching the election, they are beloved for the fathers' sakes." The rejection of the un-

believing portion of Israel is made the occasion of the
introduction of the elect among the Gentiles. Thus
the number of The Church is to be full.

Jesus rejected the secular Israel, which rejected
Him. The new Church, what Jesus called " My
Church," is the church " which by recognizing Me as
Messiah will take the place of the present Jewish
Church" (Vos, " Teaching of Jesus," p. 143). The
new church throws off the unbelief and errors of the
old church, without any loss or cessation of identity.

VIII

THE CHURCH AND THE APOSTLE PETER

VIII

THE CHURCH AND THE APOSTLE PETER

It is assumed and asserted by Roman Catholics that Jesus Christ made Peter to be the over-shepherd, and His vicar, with all His power and authority.

The antecedent improbability of Christ's doing any such thing as this is so great that it would require overwhelming proof before one could sanely believe it.

When one considers that some of these supposed vicars of Christ have been men whom Catholics themselves have regarded as children of hell, and that not one of them but has been a mere man, of human frailties, the notion that Jesus gave these men the awful power which is claimed for them seems nothing else than a form of blasphemy against Christ, even if ignorantly so.

It is necessary for the Roman Catholic church to prove three things beyond a peradventure before it can ask credence to its preposterous claim:

(1) That Christ made Peter head shepherd of His flock,

(2) That Peter had the authority from Christ to hand over his own rule to others,

(3) That in the church of Rome, and it alone, are the successors of Peter to be found.

Instead of all these statements being verified, no one of them is provable.

(1)   That Jesus made Peter over-shepherd and ruler
in The Church is commonly based on Christ's word
about the rock and the keys; and His words "feed My
sheep"; as well as on the prominence of Peter in the
apostolic circle and in the early church.

Concerning the "rock" words, these are excluded
from bearing evidence by the conclusion of the Roman
church itself at the Council of Trent, that the unani-
mous authority of the Fathers is necessary to Scripture
dogma, and the interpretation that Peter is the rock is
contradicted by the greatest of the Fathers, St. Augustine.   There is no reason for thinking that Peter is
called the rock except the play upon words which appears in the Greek, intended or unintended, but which
there is no reason to assume appeared in the Aramaic.
The translation of this sentence by Delitzch in his
Hebrew New Testament obliterates all similarity of
sound.   "Thou art Petros and upon this selah I will
build My church."

God and God alone is the Rock Foundation of The .
Church.   *It is to be noted that the foundation of the
church in the New Testament is never said to be Jesus.*
When Paul writes " other foundation can no man lay
than Christ Jesus " he refers not to The Church but to all
Christian ministry.   God is the rock, and He only and
The Church has no other foundation.   The relation
of Jesus to The Church is that of chief corner-stone;
in His own words He is " the head-stone of the cor-
ner."   (See Matt. 21 : 42; and 1 Pet. 2 : 4–6.)   In this
way all attached to Christ become, in their order, those
upon whom the subsequent edifice of The Church is

built. So Paul says that the saints are " built
foundation of the apostles and prophets, Jes
being the chief corner-stone " (Eph. 2 : 20).

In this sense, not Peter alone, but all the
and all the prophets who followed them and
are a part of the foundation, and are " builded
for an habitation of God " (Eph. 2 : 22). Pet
honourable place *near* Christ, *but not in the*
Christ. The Church is built upon God as t
not on man.

That Jesus appointed Peter head of The
when He said : " To thee I will give the ke
Kingdom of Heaven "(He says not " of the (
is contradicted by the fact that Jesus said
thing to the other apostles, and others p
Bishop Westcott maintains there were, wh
said, " Receive ye the Holy Ghost ; whoseso
ye remit they are remitted and whosesoeve
retain they are retained " (John 20 : 23). \
this means, it excludes Peter from sole prima
Church, which is our special consideration he

The same objection overthrows the not
Christ's words " Feed My sheep—My lambs
Peter supreme shepherd. That Peter is her
out is due to his recent apostasy. It is his
ment into a position he had lost. He had sh
shown himself unworthy of being a shepher
again commits to him the work of a shepherc
more than Paul did when he tells the Ephesi
to " feed the Church of God."

So also the words : " When thou art (

strengthen thy brethren" can mean, in the light of all
the facts, nothing else than that Peter after his fall and
return to Christ, will then be in a better condition than
he previously was to help his brethren.

The position of Peter in the early Church was certainly, at the outset, a prominent one, perhaps the
most prominent.   But this fact was due largely to natural gifts which made him, even during Christ's life,
the forward and even presumptuous disciple, intruding
his opinions and leaping to the front on every occasion.   Thus, Peter goes out on the water to Christ;
Peter enters the tomb where Christ's body has been;
Peter leaps into the sea to swim to Christ on the shore.
It is Peter who draws his sword and uses it.   So Peter
follows Christ into the place of trial.   It is Peter who
speaks on the Mount of Transfiguration.   It is Peter
who replies when Jesus asked who He was, and also
when the question is concerning the Temple Tax.
These suffice to explain why Peter was prominent immediately after the departure of Christ.   But, the fact
is beyond dispute that Peter did not retain this position of prominence.   He is displaced by James, the
brother of Christ, so far as Jerusalem is concerned and
by Paul so far as the Gentile world is concerned·
Although the Book of Acts seems to have as a purpose the giving to Peter a place in the early Church
which equalled that of Paul, yet this very fact shows
that Peter's place was not supreme in the early Church.
If any special evidence were needed to show that Peter
is not a solitary and supreme authority, Paul's rebuke
of Peter (Gal. 2 : 11) is sufficient.   The fact is unques-

tionable that Peter held no supreme position in the
primitive church, other than that which may be
ascribed to his natural force of character, and this position he lost as The Church extended, both in Jerusalem
and abroad. We may then safely deny that Jesus appointed Peter His successor.

(2) It is equally certain that Peter did not attempt
to hand over his authority to any successor. As there is
not a single word or fact in evidence of this we need
not waste time in chasing the shadow.

That Peter appointed a successor in Rome is a tradition without historical basis. Even those church
writers who maintain this, cannot agree as to the name
of the one whom Peter appointed, whether it was
Clement or Linus.

(3) That the Church of Rome alone possesses
those whom Peter appointed his successors is another
baseless assertion hardly worthy of a moment's attention. It is uncertain whether Peter ever was in Rome,
even though we may concede this.

That the Roman church at first looked to Peter
rather than to Paul cannot be shown. That Peter
appointed bishops nowhere else than in Rome cannot
be proven. The Roman church early took pride in
the notion, true or false, that two apostles had ministered to it. From this grew up the belief that Peter
had officiated there. The supremacy of Peter's name
came after it seemed to those looking superficially
at the gospels that Peter was originally the chief
apostle.

So far as the maintenance of the succession in Rome

is concerned, this is disproved by the many breaks in the history of the papacy. Among the many facts witnessing to this, not the least is the recent official action of the Roman Curia which takes six names off the list of popes and so reduces the number of Peter's successors, and shows the unreliable nature of this peculiar claim.

IX

THE TWELVE AND THE CHURCH

The authority in individuals or in the college.
Rome has the advantage.
Where are the churches founded by individual apostles.
No evidence of a college of the apostles.
The "Twelve" and the "Seventy."
The one text, John 20 : 21.
The "Twelve" do not fill vacancy in own ranks.
The "Twelve" a diminishing factor.
The word "apostle"; not same as "Twelve."
The early apostles not successors to the Twelve,—Paul.
The prophets in the early Church.
Hatch and Sohm quoted.
The independence of the individual churches.
The Jerusalem church not supreme in fact.
The position of James and the Jerusalem Council.
The Gentile churches Pauline not Petrine.
The Spirit ruling in the churches.
Church organization at Philippi.
Phil. 1 : 1; 1 Thess. 5 : 12; Paul's authority.
The laying on of hands.
Not an exclusive function of the "Twelve" or apostles.
Hatch quoted.

IX

THE TWELVE AND THE CHURCH

IT might have been that Jesus gave authority to the
Twelve to succeed Himself and be His vicars, which
He did not give to Peter alone.   This is the assump-
tion by many high church Anglicans.

(1)   At once a difficult question must be faced by
the Anglican catholic which the Roman claim avoids :
Was this authority vested in them as individuals or as
a college ?

That question is not considered by either Gore or
Moberly or any Anglican catholic, so far as I know.

Was each of the Twelve competent to ordain and
therefore to perpetuate an " apostolic " ministry ? or,
could they exercise this authority only as they agreed
among themselves ?

The Anglican claim goes to pieces on either horn of
this dilemma.

(a)   If it is said that each apostle can be the head
of an " apostolic " church, then we may have twelve
apostolic churches of one of which Judas Iscariot
might have been head if he had not hanged himself.
Where are these apostolic churches ?   How comes it
to pass that an " apostolic " church can perish when
Jesus gave it a ministry which was to be Himself representatively present in all authority and power?

The Roman Catholic church says that Christ gave

this authority to Peter and the Roman Catholic church exists, so it can say, argumentatively at least, in evidence of the fact. But, where is the church which owes its priesthood or ministry to James and John and Andrew and Bartholomew and all the others of the Twelve, including Mattathias? Where even is the church which owes its ministry with certainty to Paul?

Here is an extraordinary thing, that Jesus gave equal authority to twelve men, with the intention that each should perpetuate himself in the ministry, and only one of the Twelve, Peter, is claimed by any church to have done this thing, unless we consider the Chaldean claim. Surely it is shameful to credit Jesus Christ with such an abortive attempt.

(*b*) But, if it be said that it was not given to the Twelve individually to perpetuate a ministry but to them collectively we at once face the fact that there is not a scintilla of evidence that the Twelve ever constituted themselves into a body or college *to ordain successors*.

At the election of Matthias, it is distinctly said that the whole company, about one hundred and twenty, took part in the election of two men and that the lot decided between these two. There is no word that the Twelve had any more to do with the matter than any one of the other hundred members of the church (Acts 1 : 15–26). How far the Twelve exercised authority in other matters does not immediately concern us at this point.

(2) When we examine the words of Jesus upon which the supposed Anglo-catholic claim rests that

Jesus constituted the Twelve a self-perpetuating priesthood or ministry, these utterly fail to bear the tremendous pressure put upon them. We need not
again consider the words to Peter, upon which Gore
lays so much emphasis, which certainly prove nothing
as to whether Christ instituted a ministry in the person
of the Twelve and that they perpetuated it.

The work assigned to the Twelve while Christ was
on earth in the flesh, was " to preach and to have
power to heal " (Mark 3 : 14).

The authority given to the Seventy (Luke 10 : 1),
was quite similar. Matthew says " He gave them (the
Twelve) authority over unclean spirits to cast them out
and to heal all manner of diseases." He said to them,
" Go, preach, saying the Kingdom of Heaven is at
hand. Heal the sick, raise the dead, cleanse the
lepers, cast out demons " (Matt. 10 : 1–7). So far as
these words suggest, as they certainly do, the nature of
apostolic activity, there is total silence as to a self-
perpetuating authority in a church. Not one word as
to ordaining successors. It is singular that the successors of the apostles make no pretense of power to
do what is here clearly set forth and claim that about
which there is no word nor hint.

It is mainly upon one text that the Anglo-catholic
bases his belief that Jesus authorized the Twelve to perpetuate a ministry. Both Gore and Moberly rest the
high church Episcopal claims on the words : " As My
father hath sent Me, even so send I you " (John
20 : 21). What a foundation for such an immense
claim !

In the first place, to be reduced to one text as basis is to be in desperate need. Next, there is no reason for believing that these words were addressed exclusively to the Twelve. Bishop Westcott, as has been already noted, is of the opinion that others were present. This is certainly reasonable, as the words imply that all the disciples (just as in Acts 1 : 13–15) who could be, were together behind closed doors. It is also said distinctly that one of the Twelve, Thomas, was not present at this supposed time of apostolic communion and endowment.

It is also wrong to appropriate these words exclusively to the Twelve, as every one who receives the Spirit of Christ, and this is certainly the privilege of *all* believers, knows that he is Christ's vicar and has equal power with any other so to use the word of God as to bind or loose the sinner.

This was the interpretation put upon the passage in the early church. Authority is purely a matter of inspiration and this is not and never was confined to the Twelve. As Tertullian said: "It is to the spiritual man that this power is given." "The church will forgive sins, but the church of the Spirit by a spiritual man." Any other interpretation is contrary to the whole sense of New Testament teaching concerning the Spirit and the individual believer.

As Cheyne says (Art. "Binding," Ency. Biblica), "Whatsoever they (disciples) bound or loosed on earth (in expounding the law) should be bound or loosed in heaven." This was the meaning of the words as used by the Jews.

It ought to be added that the high church opinion on this subject makes the choice of Judas incomprehensible.

It must also be regarded as an extraordinary, incomprehensible thing that Jesus should have made an apostolic succession essential to the being of The Church and so, indirectly, essential to the salvation of mankind and yet not make this clear and plain.

(3) As there is no evidence that the Lord gave the Twelve the office of perpetuating a ministerial priesthood, so there is none that they exercised any such authority in The Church or that this was admitted or sought by the churches.

The relation of the Twelve to the ministry in the churches is not an obscure matter if one is willing to see the facts. And, these facts are seen in general accord by all the best scholars, including the ablest Anglicans, from Bishop Lightfoot to Dr. Sanday. On this subject the strongest anti-catholic opinions are expressed and proved by the most learned of the Anglican church.

We may call attention to certain facts which show that the Twelve did not govern the Church, nor did they appoint its ministry.

(a) The position of the Twelve was evidently one of receding authority, and was never absolute. The whole company elect two men, one of whom, selected by lot, succeeds Judas (Acts 1 : 16), and there is no mention of any apostolic influence or authority or ordination. This absence of authority in the filling of a vacancy in their own number is also seen when

no one is chosen to fill the place of James, the first of
their number to die a violent death. From the silence
on this subject, it would seem that the number, twelve,
was an ideal and not a practical fact, that the Twelve
did not regard themselves as essential to The Church.
Judas lost his ministry, but James did not, even though
deceased. He was still one of the Twelve. Had the
notion of a self-perpetuating ministry possessed the
Twelve, it is almost inconceivable that they had not
taken measures to keep their number intact, as in the
Irvingite Church. The fact is, most of the Twelve
exercised little influence in the growing Church, and
therefore little attention was paid to them as the
" Twelve." Actually the Twelve were a diminishing
factor.

This name, so common in the Gospels, is used only
once in Acts (and once in 1 Cor. 15 : 5). " The
Twelve called the multitude together" in order that
the whole church might decide a question of importance. Of the original Twelve, history tells us
almost nothing. James perished early. John lived
long, according to fairly reliable traditions. Peter's
career is involved in obscurity, though his activity
was no doubt great. Of all the others we know practically nothing. There is no evidence that any of the
Twelve appointed successors. This fact makes almost
absurd the pretension that Jesus Christ, in Gore's
words, " instituted a ministry in the person of the
Apostles" (the Twelve) and that they " perpetuated
it."

(b) The substitution of the word apostles for the

Twelve is significant. It tells that a *new* order has arisen in The Church, *displacing* the Twelve from any earlier authority they may have assumed.

The word apostle occurs once in the gospel of Matthew and six times in Luke's gospel; after that it displaces the word used most frequently in the gospels, " the Twelve."

Now these words are not synonymous and the displacement of the *name* "twelve" by the *name* " apostles " is indicative of a fact, the rise of a larger order who owed little or nothing to the original Twelve.

Not enough attention has been given to this fact, though Hort makes note of it.   There arose a superior order in The Church, distinct from and independent of the Twelve, to whom it is alleged Christ gave the perpetuation of His ministry. The break in this supposed apostolic succession is right at the beginning. The apostles of the early Church are not in succession with the Twelve. This cannot be evaded by supposing what is contrary to fact, that Paul was one of the Twelve Apostles. Paul's apostolate was only slowly and even reluctantly admitted by the " pillars " of the church (Gal. 2 : 9). It was no one of the Twelve, but an almost unknown disciple, Ananias of Damascus, who inducted Paul into the ministry. It was the church at Antioch, under direction of the Spirit, which gave Paul his apostolic commission (Acts 13: 1). Paul's claim to be an apostle took away greatly from any authority of the Twelve (including Peter) and caused at once the widening of the apostolic circle, entirely apart from any action of the original Twelve.

The word apostle became elastic, as Lightfoot first made clear. (See his "Galatians," p. 93.) Paul distinguishes, seemingly, between the Twelve and the apostles (1 Cor. 15 : 5–7). Barnabas is an apostle (Acts 14 : 4, 14 ; Gal. 2 : 9), Andronicus and Junia are apostles (Rom. 16 : 7) Silvanus is an apostle (1 Thess. 2 : 6), and Timothy. Epaphroditus is so named (Phil. 2 : 25). So are Titus and others (2 Cor. 8 : 23). Later use of the term in the Didache testifies to the fact that it named those who went forth in the *Spirit* as missionaries to *extend* the Church, rather than to minister to it, though this latter was, of course, not excluded. As missionaries, they differed from the prophets who ministered to the churches.

(*c*) The position and authority of the prophets in the early Church is another fact which tells us that the Twelve, as well as later apostles, held no supreme position in the Church, so far as the ministry was concerned. While the apostles are named before the prophets, yet this does not actually put the prophet in a subordinate place, since the apostle was simply a prophet of unusual spiritual power and a broader ministry. The place of the prophet in the early Church has only been recognized in recent years. Hatch has called attention to it, and Sohm has made clear that the Word of God, as spoken by a prophet, was the one supreme authority in the Church. Indeed, the plain fact is that the Holy Spirit is the one recognized authority in the Acts and in the history of the Church for a century and a half after Christ. This was what Jesus had promised, so the Church believed.

It was especially through the prophets that the Holy
Spirit spoke. Paul gloried in his gift of prophecy.
Indeed, as Saul, he was numbered among the prophets
(Acts 13 : 1). So also is Barnabas. The later
apostolate was born out of the prophetic order, and no
apostle was independent of the word of the prophets.
" It seemed good to the Holy Spirit and to us," says
the Jerusalem Council. The prophets represented the
Holy Ghost, the one supreme authority in the Church.

The growth of prophecy, and of its power, which
Harnack calls despotic, the conflicts with the regular
ministry, the overthrow of Montanism, which Hatch
describes, fittingly, as the " beating of the wings of
pietism against the iron bars of organization," the
crushing of prophetism by Episcopacy,—these are
facts of Church history which tell us that not to the
Twelve, nor even to later apostles, so much as to the
prophets, the Church looked for its ministry.

(*d*) The independence of the individual churches
of any authority exercised by the original Twelve
Apostles is a fact which is in need of no special pene-
tration for its recognition. The apostles remained at
Jerusalem (Acts 8: 1) and so had no personal part in
the beginning of the churches outside of Judea. The
visit of Peter and John to Samaria was, possibly, an
attempt to extend the control or direction of the
mother church in Jerusalem over the children springing up in other parts of the land. But all that the
apostles Peter and John did was to pray for them and
to lay hands on them so that they received the Holy
Ghost. The church at Antioch is visited by Barnabas,

but he does nothing there except to exhort the brethren and to preach the gospel. There is no suggestion of organization. The independence of the Antioch church is seen in their sending forth Barnabas and Paul on their apostolic mission. In this, the greatest Church movement ever undertaken since Christ's life on earth, the Jerusalem church and the Twelve are not consulted. Indeed the story of this mission gives us knowledge of the fact that it was hardly if at all acceptable to the church at Jerusalem.

Paul and Barnabas report again to the church at Antioch (Acts 14: 27) and had no intention of going to Jerusalem at all. It was only when men from Jerusalem came and disturbed the peace of the church that it seemed advisable for Paul and Barnabas to go up to Jerusalem. But Paul went not to secure any commendation from the Apostles at Jerusalem. He went to present his side of the great Gentile question. The famous Council at Jerusalem (Acts 15) shows not an Apostle, not one of the Twelve, but James, the Lord's brother, in the chair. The position of James in the Jerusalem church has always been a cross to the advocates of an apostolic episcopal succession. That the Twelve appointed him is an unfounded guess. The fact is almost certain that he was chosen to the position of an archisynagogos because of his blood relationship to Jesus. This is what Eusebius seems to say, and is generally accepted as the fact.

This Council was a popular assembly of Christians. " All the multitude," it is said, " held their peace " (15 : 22). The elders were probably, as Hort says,

elder brethren at the head of a great family of
brethren. In this assembly the Twelve exercise no
control. James expresses his opinion and it has
weight. The decision reached is a matter which the
council advises, but does not command. As Hort
says (p. 82), there are many words used in Greek to
express command, yet not one of these is used. The
word dogma is an elastic word and means, so Hort
says, no more than a resolution. While Paul, at the
outset of his next tour, delivers this opinion in good
faith, yet the speedy silent ignoring of it tells plainly
enough that the apostles at Jerusalem are *not* the head
of The Church, though Peter and James are there.

The result of this conference was but slight. For a
short time it served to allay differences. But Christians were actually divided into two antagonistic
portions. Paul and Barnabas took the Gentile world
and James and Peter and John took the Jewish world
(Gal. 2 : 7–12). This fact is, by the way, against any
Petrine influence in the church at Rome, which was
Pauline. Peter's ministry is declared to be among
Jews, not Gentiles. This council, which sought to
satisfy the legalistic Christians and to put an end to
interference with Paul's work (Acts 15 : 1) did not
fully succeed in its purpose. Paul was constantly
harassed by the " Jewish party." Yet, it ended all
official or organized interference and virtually acknowledged the independence of the Gentile churches.
It is a matter of fact that " the Twelve" made no assertion of any authority over Pauline churches.

(*e*) All the churches outside of Syria, of which we

know anything, were Pauline churches. Not that
he planted them all, but that he fathered them
all (1 Thess. 2:11; 1 Cor. 4:15). Even the Roman
church was Pauline, as Paul's letter, and his desire to
visit Rome show, since he made it a rule not to build
on another man's foundation. Its Pauline character
is also evidenced in his letters from Rome, showing
Paul's personal relation to its leading members and
their attachment to him.

Since it is beyond dispute that no other apostle,
and no outside church, not Jerusalem nor even
Antioch, exercised domination over these churches,
then only Paul can be looked to as the apostle who
gave " holy orders," instituted the Christian ministry in
these churches. John, the apostle, came long after
Paul to Ephesus, and his work there is traditional
rather than historical. If Peter was ever at Rome, it
was after the church had been under the hands of
Paul.

If Paul did not organize these churches, then the
inference is assured that they organized themselves.

The reasons for believing that Paul did not fix the
ministry of these churches may be briefly stated.

From the Pauline epistles it is made very evident
that the churches of the uncircumcision were essentially and fully theocratic. There was but one
authority recognized, that of the Holy Spirit. All
those who ministered in any wise in these churches
did so by virtue of spiritual gifts. This Paul teaches
in his letters to the Corinthians, to the Romans, and
to the Ephesians.

The spirit was given to *all* and not to some, but in difference of kind. Therefore the ministry was, originally, a spiritually spontaneous rather than an externally ordered ministry. From the apostle down to the humblest servant in The Church, the place of each was determined by his use of spiritual gifts, and The Church must " try the spirits." There were apostles, prophets, teachers; there were those who had power, could heal; there were helps, governments, tongues (1 Cor. 12 : 28).

In writing to the Romans (12:6–8) Paul mentions such ministrations as " prophecy, service, teaching, giving, ruling." In Ephesians (4: 11) there are " apostles, prophets, evangelists, pastors, teachers." *In no one of these lists is there any mention of such an official as a presbyter, or bishop, or deacon.*

Beside the fact of dependence upon immediate spiritual direction, there was another fact which hindered any early demand for organization,—that the expectation was universal in The Church of a speedy termination of mundane conditions through the advent of Christ and the Kingdom of God. This removed from the minds of the earliest Christians any pressure towards a fixity of church ministry.

These two facts explain why there appears no church government in the earliest times. There are no officials appealed to, to exercise authority in the church at Corinth. Paul appeals to the customs prevailing in other churches, to *their common-sense.* " Doth not nature teach you?" He asserts his own authority as their father, as their teacher, as one who

has as much right as any one to be called an apostle.
He will "set things in order when he comes." Paul
does not in his salutations and references give any
reason to believe that there were officials of a permanent sort. Phil. 1 : 1 is hardly an exception. Paul,
while dictating, as Schmiedel suggests, suddenly re-
members that there are episcopoi and diakonoi at
Philippi. Yet, their place is *after* the "saints" and
not before them. These are still servants, not lords,
of the church. But, this letter is certainly a late one
among Paul's letters, and therefore this first allusion to
bishops (elders as Lightfoot translates) and deacons
suggests that at Philippi, just where we would expect
it, in this Roman city, we have *the beginning of the
growth of a permanent ministry*. Before this, the
only suggestion of an officer is as to those who pre-
sided at the meetings (1 Thess. 5 : 12), almost certainly
the elders (1 Tim. 5 : 17). The necessary inference
from the New Testament writings as well as other
early Christian writings is that during the lifetime
of the Twelve (and Paul) church government was in a
fluid condition, plastic, not fixed. Here and there a
church, as at Philippi, was getting into shape. But the
government was self-determined and only sporadically
assisted by a messenger sent by the Apostle Paul. So
far as the bishops (elders) and deacons were rising into
fixedness of service, Paul claims no authority and
never speaks of ordaining, or transmitting holy orders
to any one. The passage in Acts 14 : 23, as even Gore
admits, does not tell of ordination, but merely of
election of elders, which Paul and Barnabas directed.

There is no hint of anything beyond the election of
elders.   When Paul speaks of laying hands on
Timothy, which he did in apparent connection with
the elders of some church (not of a modern presbytery), there is no implication that here was any induc-
tion into an office, but simply into a service.   Timothy
was the helper of Paul, his fellow missionary, a fellow
apostle.   Of ordinations at all in the later sense there
were none in apostolic times; Dr. Hatch has shown
this beyond a doubt.

When Dr. Gore asks (p. 357), " Could any Christian
receive the Holy Spirit except by the laying on of
apostolic hands," it is easy enough to point to Pentecost,
and to the assembly mentioned in Acts 4 : 31, and to
Cornelius as well, or to the many cases when prophets
spake by the Holy Spirit.   Gore's notion that the
Holy Spirit is given only to such as have hands laid
on them by apostles (or their successors) is contradicted by the fact that God gives His spirit to all His
children who have faith (John 7 : 38).   As Paul says
to the Galatians, " received ye the Spirit by the works
of the law or by the hearing of faith ? " (3 : 2).   The
Spirit comes in answer to prayer and faith.

This laying on of hands, except among the superstitious, has never meant anything more than a significant gesture, an outward sign, by which there was indicated some attitude, mental or spiritual, of the one
giving to another receiving.   The hand itself is the
significant member of the body, and gives indication
of what is in the heart or mind of a person.   It is
lifted against another in wrath, towards him in favour,

over him in blessing. So far as ordination or installation is concerned it means no more than a blessing
conferred, which is actually conferred only so far as
God sanctions the wish or prayer in the heart of the
one ordaining. So far as office is concerned, ordination is merely recognition, and an installation. There
is no inward necessity for ordination. It is an official
recognition by the church, large or small, through its
leaders, of some one as member or minister of a
church, and so is a setting apart as member or minister. To say that it is a mere form does not deny its
value. For forms have value, and are not lightly to be
set aside. Yet, of apostolic ordination the New Testament knows little or nothing.

It was a number of " prophets and teachers " who
laid hands on " Barnabas and Saul " for their missionary work. Thus Barnabas was made an apostle not
by apostles but by the church represented by
" prophets and teachers " at Antioch. The gift of the
Holy Ghost is associated in Acts sometimes with this
hand-laying, but not always. The few instances in
Acts when the apostles' hands brought the Holy
Ghost do not justify the inference either that the
Holy Ghost was only conferred in that way or that it
was the exclusive right of the apostles to lay-on
hands. There are but seven instances in the New
Testament of this ceremony; of these, two only may
refer to the original Twelve. Acts 6: 6 is not certainly
an exclusive apostolic ordination. There is no reason
for excluding the elders from participation in it. The
other case is Acts 8: 17, where there was no ordination

but a simple confirmation. Once Paul lays hands on disciples that they may receive the Holy Ghost (Acts 19:6). He also lays hand on Timothy in connection with the presbytery (1 Tim. 4:14; 2 Tim. 1:6). In the other cases a common disciple lays hands on Paul (Acts 9:17); the prophets and teachers lay hands on Barnabas and Saul and so constitute them apostles so far as man could do that. But the apostles at Jerusalem had nothing to do with it. It was an act of the *Church* by means of those prophets and teachers (Acts 13:3). Timothy is told not to lay hands suddenly on any one (1, 5:22). It is pretty certain (see Huther Com.) that this does not refer to ordination to office. The context decides against this. " Lay not hands in a hasty fashion on any one, *neither* be partaker of other men's sins; keep thyself pure." And (in v. 20), " Them that sin rebuke before all that others may fear." Titus (1:5) is told to " ordain elders in every city " (in Crete). But the word translated *ordain* here is, *kathistemai*, which carries merely the idea of placing, and must have been with the consent of the churches. It was what Paul and Silas did in Iconium (Acts 14:23), where the word is to elect, or have elected, and not ordain. (See Gore, p. 257. Cf. Stephanus Thes. Græcæ Linguæ.)

What concerns us is that these functionaries were not appointed by the apostles, nor ordained by the apostles, according to any evidence we possess. It was in the Church that the authority reposed. The words of Hatch (" Organization of the Early Church,"

p. 130ff.) on the subject of ordination are conclusive: —

(1) All the words which are in use to express appointment to ecclesiastical rank connote either simple appointment or accession to rank.

(2) All these words were in use to express appointment to civil office. When other ideas than those of civil appointment came beyond question to attach themselves to ecclesiastical appointment, other words were used. The absence of such words in the earlier period of itself affords a strong presumption of the absence of the ideas which are relative to them.

(3) There were the same elements in appointment to both civil and ecclesiastical office: nomination, election, approval by a presiding officer.

(4) All the modes of admission to ecclesiastical office were, with one exception, analogous to the modes of admission to civil office. Hatch shows that the elected one simply entered on to the duty of his office. Imposition of hands was not regarded as essential. So far as practiced, it was always accompanied by prayer. Augustine resolves it into a prayer: "*quid aliud est manuum impositio quam oratio super hominem*" (Hatch, p. 132).

Hatch shows that " ordination " was not supposed to confer special or spiritual favours. He argues this from silence upon a matter extremely important; from the facility with which ordination was made and unmade.

Therefore, we conclude, the evidence is strongly

against the opinion that Paul transmitted authority to those who ruled in the churches of the western world.

If Paul did not, certainly no other prophet or apostle ever did.

X

THE CHURCH AND THE PRIESTHOOD
OF ISRAEL

Can organization be inferred from the Old Testament ?
The worship of God not priestly.
The Levitical régime not essential to Israel.
Neither circumcision nor passover priestly performances.
The priest inferior to the prophet.
Melchizedek and Christ.
The " priest " ignored in the New Testament.
Christ not followed by priests but prophets, pastors.

X

THE CHURCH AND THE PRIESTHOOD
OF ISRAEL

It may, however, be said that as God appointed
ministers and ordained a priesthood for His people
under the earlier dispensation, therefore we may conclude that He did so under the later, and that Jesus
did appoint those who should be the shepherds of His
flock when He Himself should be no longer visible in
the flesh among them.

This statement has affected, even decided, many
who have not sufficiently scrutinized the subject. It
raises two questions of fact: (1) Did God, in the
earlier dispensation, ordain a priesthood which, in
perpetuity, should constitute *the form without which
there could be no substance* of a covenant people?
(2) Did Jesus in anticipation of His departure hand
over, in perpetuity, the shepherding of His flock to
the apostles and their successors?

(1) The affirmation of the first question does not
affirm the second, on the contrary it denies it. It
would simply mean that the Pontifex Maximus of the
later must be in succession with the High Priest of
the earlier dispensation.

The relation of the priesthood of the Jewish church
to the true Israel of God is not of an essential nature,
like that maintained to be the case in the " catholic "

church.   Even though we admit, what however is not so true as it seems to be, that the priesthood, the hierarchy, which controlled the worship of Israel was directly originated by God Himself, rather than begotten, as priesthood always has been among other nations, of impulses and weaknesses which possess the larger part of mankind, yet *the mere fact that God gave to a hierarchy the conduct of the worship of Israel* (if He did) *did not condition the existence of Israel, nor was it ever an essential factor.*   " It is a false assumption that the external Israel was the true Israel " (Charles Hodge, " Church Polity," p. 65).

It is certain that Israel existed as a people of God centuries before there was the priesthood which may be traced, but not uninterruptedly, to Aaron or Moses.

It is certain that the worship of God was never restricted to the office of the priests.   After the origin, according to orthodox or catholic opinion, of the priesthood and the levitical order, the kings and the prophets, as well as heads of families, worshipped God in a free fashion.

To say that the priests and Levites were essential to Israel is to ignore the most patent facts of Old Testament history.

As the domination of Mosaic Law is regarded by Paul as a mere episode of transient and doubtful advantage, even more so was the domination of the priesthood, even though its origin might be, like the Law, traced by those who adored it, to the immediate agency of God.

It is a fact of widest significance that the two ceremonies which most anciently seemed to hold Israel
together as one people, were not dependent on the
priesthood, namely the rite of circumcision and the
passover. That these two modes of worship of God,
are not peculiar to Israel is well known. It is also true
that the administration, in early Israel as in later
Judaism, did not require priestly assistance.

Circumcision was practiced long before the Jewish
priesthood came into existence, and after the priesthood, was practiced entirely apart from any priestly
interference. It was and it is, a family or tribal matter.
The circumciser is generally either a professional
mohel, or the father ; and the place may be a synagogue or it may be a private house. This rite,
which introduced, visibly into Israel, and which became
the fleshly mark of an Israelite and so was the rite
which really gave to Israel visible existence, was in no
wise dependent on a priesthood.

Equally true was the passover a family and a
national affair before and after the priesthood was living fact. It is certain that the passover did not
originate with Moses, even though it acquired new
significance just as it acquired new significance under
the Christian dispensation. But no priest was necessary to the observance of the passover, neither in
early Christian times was a priest thought necessary
for the correct observance of the " supper."

It must further be noted that the prophet in Israel
took precedence of the priest just as in the apostolic
church the prophets were first.

The inferior position of the priest in Israel is attested by a hundred passages. The relative uselessness of his services and his sacrifices, often the utter repudiation of the priests and their worship, is the frequent theme of the prophets. Whether or not the priests maintained an unbroken succession is, therefore, of little importance.

It may be safely said that if the priesthood had been of value Jesus Christ would have come in priestly succession. (See Hebrews 7 : 14.) As it was, He came in the succession of the prophets, through John the Baptist. Though John was a priest's son he never fulfilled any priestly duty. Whether Jesus had anything to do with the priests or their services is to be answered in the negative rather than in the affirmative. These were among the first to reject Him.

Of duty to the priest Jesus speaks but once. He tells a man healed of leprosy to go to one and secure the priestly certificate of his healing. In this case the priest acted as a public health officer whose testimony was necessary if the man healed was to be received again into the community. (See also Luke 10 : 30 ff.)

When the author of the Hebrews, who addresses those inclined to priestism, would show that Jesus was priest, it is significant that he goes back to Melchizedek, who represents a racial priesthood, while Aaron, with his succession, is ignored.

Without further words, then, we can surely and safely say that even if the Aaronic priesthood were due to a "thus saith the Lord" in all respects, rather than to mixed motives partly of God and partly of man's own weakness and superstitiousness, yet it was never more than an incident, an accident, and no wise essential to the existence of Israel as the true church of God.

(2) The second inference sometimes drawn is that Jesus must have given His flock into the care of shepherds, who receiving their authority from Him, passed it on to others. It is said, Jesus would not send forth His sheep without a shepherd. On this purely a priori ground it is concluded that The Church cannot exist without a priesthood, apostolic in origin and succession.

Before inquiring into the matter of fact, it may be suggested that this idea has less bearing on apostolic succession than may seem to be the case.

It may be noted that God's sheep of the old dispensation were, as we have said, much better pastured by prophets whom God raised up than they were by the priests. How many priests fed the flock of Israel of whom mention is made in the Old Testament? Is there one? But of prophets we know of many. Therefore we might conclude that God has committed the sheep who are Christ's flock not to priests who fatten on them, but to prophets who feed them.

And this inference from the Old Dispensation is abundantly verified by the facts of the New, and the priesthood which has usurped authority in the New Dispensation is much like that of the Old. That God has committed the flock of Christ to prophets is clear enough from the fact that *never once in the New Testament is any minister called a priest, nor any priestly duty ascribed to any minister.*

But prophetical succession, in all the history of Israel and God's Church, has always been a matter of the Spirit and not of form.   Prophets may recognize one another and recommend one another and help one another and agree among one another; but a prophet is from God direct.   There is no succession of prophets.   Paul had no successor, nor Luther, nor Wesley. All which the Church, that is God's children, Christ's flock, can do, is to recognize the prophets, try the spirits.

It is, then, fact that even when the " Great Shepherd of the Sheep" is taken away from the sight of the flock, Christ will not leave them orphans, shepherdless. He sends the Spirit of truth, the Paraclete, who leads unto all truth.   The *Holy Spirit is, therefore, the one Shepherd of Christ's flock*, and He guides by means of all those whom He inspires to lead the flock of God. It has ever been the custom of The Church to look to such for guidance and the life of The Church is dependent upon its recognition of true shepherds and its detection of those who are wolves, false shepherds.

We can safely conclude that Jesus Christ was succeeded, not by priests, but by pastors.   The Church is to be served by ministers whom God endows with His Spirit, and whom a church recognizes and accepts.

THE SELF-ORGANIZATION OF THE CHURCHES

Spiritual gifts.

Organization necessary for order in church.

The " Seven." Lindsay's opinion criticised.

McGiffert's opinion.

That the " Seven " were elders.

The Jerusalem church not distinctly organized.

The Jerusalem Christians as the true Israel.

Elders elected under supervision of church founders.

Was there a " bishop " over these churches.

1 Thess. 5: 12; Rom. 16: 1–3.

First use of episcopos.

Relation of deacon and bishop. Réville.

Both deacons and elders perform episcopal functions.

Was the elder an official? Opinions.

Hatch and Schmiedel as to episcopal duties.

In Acts 20, the elders perform episcopal duties.

The Didache. Clement. 1 Timothy.

The Church at Antioch long prophetic.

Church organization first at Philippi.

No threefold order recognizable in Paul's letters.

This first in Ignatian letters.

A presbyterial church.

XI

THE SELF-ORGANIZATION OF THE CHURCHES

THAT the organization of the primitive churches (we have seen that there was no one organized church) was not effected by the Apostles or their successors in response to authority given them by Jesus Christ, is further seen when we consider *the process of the organization of these churches and the evolution of the bishop*. It was a natural process. This does not exclude the influence of the Spirit.

We have already seen that there is no evidence of apostolic interference or appointment. At the outset, the churches, so we must conclude from Paul's letters, were under the direction of those who had spiritual gifts. Whether or not there was any mistake in the judgment as to the Spirit's working is not of any moment here. The fact is indisputable: the Spirit, working in apostles and prophets and teachers and helpers and miracle workers and ecstatically awakened ones, was the only recognized governor of the local church. That such a condition could not continue permanently is self-evident. There arose disorders in the church at Corinth. Yet it is very significant that Paul does not suggest the election or appointment of an official board. He simply gives suggestions as to the regulation of the spiritual gifts. All must be done decently and in order. No one will, probably, question that the meetings of the early churches resembled a popular prayer-meeting, as in a Methodist church.

When, where, and how did organization begin?

As already said, it is not uncommon to answer that this organization began under the direction of the Apostles when "the Seven" are installed to attend to the "ministry of tables" at Jerusalem.

Dr. Lindsay says: "This earliest example of church organization contains in it three interesting elements—apostolic guidance and sanction; the independence of the community, and, as a result, a representative system of administration" (pp. 117–118).

But this is inaccurate. There is no evidence for, and much against, the assumption that these seven were permanent officers in the Jerusalem church. If their office was permanent, what was it? They were not deacons in the later sense. That is quite generally admitted. They were not called so until after the second century. They are not called deacons by Luke nor by any other New Testament writer, and, as McGiffert says: "there is no sign that there were ever deacons in the church of Jerusalem" (p. 77). Lightfoot ("Christian Ministry") says the seven were deacons. His arguments are, however, unsatisfactory. He says the functions are substantially the same; that though the word deacon does not occur the verb *diakonein* does; that the emphasis St. Luke puts on the appointment shows that St. Luke regards the appointment as permanent. But the functions discharged by the seven were not identical with those of the deacons

who were, later, the assistants of the bishops in their
work and had no peculiar work of their own. The
use of the verb diakonein does not signify that these
men were deacons, because exactly this verb is used
to designate the work of the apostles in this very connection. *The apostles were " deacons of the word," the
seven were appointed to be " deacons of tables."* As to
the permanency of the office, the seven ceased almost
immediately to attend to the tables, and the only two
who figure at all in Acts are the evangelist Philip, who
does the work of an apostle, and Stephen, who also
was eminently a preacher of the gospel. Further,
when later (Acts 11 : 30) the church at Antioch sends
an alms to the church at Jerusalem, it is *sent to the
elders, and not to deacons.* Against the identification
of the seven with the deacons is also the fact which
Lightfoot proves, and which Gwatkin (Hastings's Dict.)
also asserts, that there was no corresponding office in
the Levitical order, nor was it taken from the synagogue. That the diaconate spread to the Gentile
churches is just a reversal of the fact. *It originated in
the Gentile churches.*

That the seven were presbyters or elders is true
only so far as the elders meant old or dignified men.
In an official sense we have no good reason for
identifying the seven with presbyters, even though
this is the opinion of Ritschl and has been adopted
by not a few, including Lindsay. It is safest and
surest to say, with McGiffert, that the seven were a
committee, serving only a temporary purpose, and
that the duties entrusted to them were later assumed

by the elders. In favour of this is the fact that the occasion of their appointment, the early communism, was transient, and also that they are never mentioned again. They have no place in the Council of Jerusalem (Acts 15).

Does the Jerusalem church show itself to be organized at all? The answer must be, it does not. The fact is, that the Jerusalem Christians continued to be Israelites, so long as there was a Jerusalem community of Christians, that is until 70 A. D. It is superfluous to argue this. It is enough simply to adduce that when Paul last visited Jerusalem he was induced to show that even he had not totally abandoned Judaism, and for the sake of peace he compromised his original position and suffered for it with imprisonment and death. The Jerusalem Christians were against Paul, because his Christianity was a bridge for the Jews to cross over to the Gentiles, rather than for the Gentiles to become Jews. In Jerusalem the Christians were a kind of a synagogue with James at the head, and with him the elders, and of organization as a church separate from Israel there is not a hint. The Christians there regarded themselves as the true Israel. Until the destruction of Jerusalem, they continued (as we see in Acts 3: 1; 21: 20) in the religious customs of their fathers, including worship in the temple, the practice of circumcision, and the observance of legal traditions. When compelled to flee from Jerusalem they, as might be expected, organized themselves, with Symeon, a cousin of Jesus, at their head. With this appointment the apostles had nothing to do. Therefore we must abandon Jerusalem as giving any suggestion as to when and where and how the later church organization began and progressed. And this takes us out of the influence of the " Twelve " Apostles.

Can we find in the words that Paul and Barnabas saw to the choice of " elders in all the churches " the indication of church organization? As has already been stated, Paul and Barnabas did not in any technical sense " *ordain* elders in every church." What Luke says is, as is now generally conceded, that Paul and Barnabas superintended an election of elders. From this it would appear that the administration of the affairs of the churches in Asia Minor (for we may include Ephesus) was committed to a single board or committee of elders whose duty it was to watch over —episcopein—the church and feed it (Acts 20: 28). As to the number of elders or their special duties we are not informed. It is probable that both were undefined, and it is certain that the duties were not to conflict with the free exercise of spiritual gifts. Yet, even this being accepted as a fact does not fully answer our question. A company of Christians under the leadership of a committee or board of elders is not an organized church in the later sense. Besides, there is no evidence from Paul's epistles, nor any further evidence from Acts, that even this presbytery was common to all the churches. (Timothy was probably ordained at Lystra by the elders and Paul, Acts 16: 3.) In no letter (except Philippians) does Paul allude to such a body in any other church. The silence is certainly significant when both politeness as well as usefulness would naturally demand reference to such officers.

The first and only mention is in the salutation addressed to the Philippians. Here, we learn, there were " bishops and deacons." Can we find any earlier hints? All the churches had in them some leading men and women. Paul's salutations prove this. In no case is any one person given an official title. It is never bishop or elder so and so, nor deacon so and so. Yet, it is also plain that some men and women occupied positions which were virtually official. That is, their duties were becoming permanent. Stephanus had great influence; but this was because he and his household " devoted themselves to the ministry of the saints " (1 Cor. 16 : 15). He is not called, however, a deacon nor an elder. In Romans 12 : 8 and 1 Thessalonians 5 : 12 there is mention of the proistamenoi. In the opinion of Hatch and Hort and Lindsay, these are the patrons of the Christian community. But Réville thinks they could not have held such a conspicuous position, as they were not well known.

Hort says ("Ecclesia," p. 126): " It is morally impossible that proistamenos can here (1 Thess. 5 : 12) be a technical term for an office, standing as it does between ' labouring ' and ' admonishing.' " Phœbe held a high place as servant (diakonos) of the church at Cenchrea (Rom. 16 : 1-3).

It will probably bring the situation before us if we represent to ourselves a community of Christians who, while exercising their spiritual gifts with liberty (Gal.

5 : 1), yet recognize the seniority and dignity of some among them who are called proistamenoi or hegemenoi or kubernesoi. These are those who perform diakonia and are called presbuteroi, both in the Greek and the Jewish churches. It is in the Gentile churches, to begin with, that the word episcopos comes into use as designating the highest service of the elders.

The question as to whether the two orders, deacon and bishop, appeared simultaneously or separately had better, probably, be answered by saying that the earliest official class recognized in the churches were the seniors, the elders, the oldest men or the oldest Christians, and that these performed, at first with no special distinction, the duties which were necessary in the congregation, which duties are designated diaconal and episcopal. The *diaconal services were certainly performed by elders*, if the New Testament use of the word deacon means anything.

Réville says (p. 149): "The analysis of texts which concern the deacons shows clearly that there was *no organization of an order of deacons* in the primitive communities on pagan soil, but it shows that there was a *category of members* who, in virtue of the functions they filled in the service of the church, are called deacons." Yet this category would easily become fixed and official.

Lindsay says, expressively and truly, "services crystallized into offices" (p. 143).

But it is also possible that the earliest *deacons, servants, of the church were called in Macedonia, episcopoi,*

even though their work is called a diakonia. Hatch
and Réville have endeavoured to show that this name
episcopos was common to designate an official class
both in municipalities and in societies.

Timothy is called " deacon of God " (1 Thess. 3 : 2).
Paul and Apollos are " deacons through whom ye believed " (1 Cor. 3 : 5). Paul says, " I glory in my
diaconate " (Rom. 11 : 13). He calls himself a deacon
of the gospel (Eph. 3 : 7) and of the church (Col. 1 : 24).
There are many other instances.

That the elders performed episcopal service is distinctly stated in Acts 20. That is, the elders did both
diakonein and episkopein.

That these services should become more and more
distinct is natural, and those who performed services
called diaconal would be called deacons, and that those
who performed the service episcopal would be named
bishops. Thus the two orders would arise at once by
separation of the elders into two classes. This being
so, there is truth in the contention that *some elders
called deacons might be inferior to some other elders
called bishops. And the word elder ceases to be a
synonym with the word bishop, although every bishop
was, originally, an elder, a presbyter.*

Out of this multiplicity of services and functions, we
see emerging a local presbytery (Acts 20 : 17–35).
The pastoral office, or the transferring to some one of
special duties, is a gradual and inevitable development
of service. An elder who distinguished himself, or
who was distinguished in the possession of spiritual
gifts, would naturally come to preëminence. This

elder would be the chief overseer of the flock, and the name of his *duty* would become the name of his *office*. There were many elders. This was the common name. The name of the most esteemed function, oversight, would belong specially to him who exercised this function.

The researches of Hatch, supplemented by Harnack and Réville, show that the episcopos, or the epimelete, was a specially distinguished servant or officer in societies of that period, in the Græco-Roman world. The name episcopos, or bishop, therefore, took precedence of the name elder.

In the opinion of Hatch, Harnack, Sohm, Réville, McGiffert, A. V. G. Allen, and others, the elder, or presbyter, was not an official, he was an old man, or one whose dignity and weight was equal to that of an old man, and who simply for that reason exercised influence and authority. These do not, all, identify the elder and the bishop. In the opinion of Lightfoot, Lindsay, Loening, Loofs, Schmiedel, Sanday and others, the elder was an official and was originally identical with the bishop, that is, exercised episcopal functions.

From what has already been said, our opinion is that the terms elder and bishop are not synonymous, because the elders were called in to do deacons' service. In favour of this opinion is, further, the fact that *deacons are said to advance to the episcopal office and not to the presbyterate.* " They who have served well as deacons gain to themselves a good standing " (1 Tim. 3 : 13). " Those who have served well as deacons purchase to themselves the pastorate" (Apos. Canons, 21).

Also, presbyters and deacons are not associated together in a church, but bishops and deacons.

But this matter is not essential to our inquiry, however interesting, and the reader will find the matter discussed in the encyclopedias and by many able writers. Lindsay (p. 157 ff.) gives a summary of the arguments.

What were the special duties of the deacon and the bishop do not concern us, but the bishop had the chief duties and the deacon was his assistant. Robertson says (Ency. Biblica, "Bishop"): "We may say that New Testament evidence points to the existence of two classes of administration: a class of rulers and more humble servants."

The episcopate and the diaconate are derived from the one original eldership, whether as official or merely honourary.

The fact that the deacons came to perform a secondary service, would naturally bring it about that the younger men would be selected for this office and the older men for the episcopal office. Thus, though at the outset the older ones, i. e., elders, filled both offices, they would later fill only the higher. Thus it came about that later in the church the presbuteros and the episcopos *were* identical. It is only on the basis of this later identity that we can explain the use of the word presbyter when the episcopos became supreme. The episcopoi are selected, later, only from the elders. When there came to be, in the second century, a *single* episcopos in a church, by way of eminence, this left others still recognized as elders, presbyters, in the church.

Hatch would make episcopal duties chiefly eleemosynary. He certainly adduces considerable evidence, but, as Schmiedel has shown, the duty of a bishop was also to "shepherd," to teach, to preside.

Those who were made bishops and deacons, Clement of Rome tells us, were the *first fruit*, that is, the earliest converts of the apostle (Cf. Paul's letter, 1 Cor. 16: 15). These Clement also calls " elders " and these elders in Clement's day presented at the altar the gifts at the celebration of the supper or communion, thus showing that in Clement's time (95 A. D.) the bishop had not yet reached the position in Corinth he attained at Antioch in the days of Ignatius (120–150 A. D.).

When Acts 20 was written it is clear that the elders if not officially bishops (because this office was then unknown) yet performed episcopal duties.

When the Didache was written, which tells a church to elect bishops and deacons, it is clear that the plurality of bishops was not altogether a thing of the past. That is, a number of elders did episcopal duty in one church. The date of the Didache can only be inferred, but this direction of itself makes it probable that it was written early in the second century, before the Ignatian letters in which one bishop appears in a church, not several as in the Didache and in Philippians 1 : 1.

This condition of affairs where each church had a plural number of both bishops and deacons cannot have lasted very long, although it is difficult to set any date for the rise of the single bishop in the Church. There is difficulty in reconciling 1 Timothy with Clement's letter. From Clement's letter to Corinth, written about 95, it would appear that in Corinth, at least, there were still a plural number of bishops in that church. "It is a pity to turn such out of their episcopate," he says, and adds, "blessed are those *elders* who have gone before" and are therefore safe from such treatment. In chapter forty-seven he speaks of the conflict in the church as against the presbyters, and in chapter fifty-four he says, "let the flock of Christ be at peace along with the elders," and chapter fifty-seven, "Do ye who began this sedition submit yourselves to the elders." Here we find a plural number of elders or bishops in one church.

In 1 Timothy, it would seem as though a single elder or bishop was over the church. We must assume either that 1 Timothy was written later, in the second century, or else that the movement towards a single bishop proceeded more rapidly in other places than in Corinth, this being an exceptionally disorderly city.

It is certain that organization would not commence in any church until there began to be a transition from the prophetic to the regular ministry, not until what Paul predicts began to take place, when "tongues shall cease."

Wherever in a church there was first apparent a cessation of spiritual emotion and also a distinct feeling of the need of order, there would first appear the transition from the pure theocracy or prophetic rule, to the rule of a local sub-prophetic government. There was gain in this, but it was also fraught with evil. Antioch seems to have remained prophetic longer than some other churches. Its full organization came suddenly. (See the Epistles of Ignatius.) It was certainly not in Asia Minor, as here was the home of Montanism and where the prophets longer retained sway. The letters to " Ephesus " and " Colossus " show this, as also does the book of " Revelation."

We would expect to find the first indication in a Græco-Roman community. Here reason, and desire for order, would soon assert themselves. That there were those in these churches whose influence was becoming authoritative is made clear from the Epistles to the Thessalonians, to Rome, and to Philippi. Corinth furnishes an exception, as might be expected from the nature of that city, which was more Oriental and less Roman. In Corinth, when Paul writes, it is evident that authority rests in the whole church (1 Cor. 5 : 3). There are indeed kuberneseis in the church (12 : 28), yet the duty of these is probably monitory. That the proistamenoi and kuberneseis and poimenes are not head officials is seen (Réville, p. 143) in that they are named at the end of the lists.

From our general knowledge of the facts, it is not unreasonable to suppose that church organization, as it later developed, was more advanced in Macedonia than elsewhere, and that at Philippi the initiative of the later episcopal government of the Church was taken. Here there were few Jews, as Réville shows,

(p. 148, note), and therefore a Græco-Roman development would be expected. Though poor, the church
is an example of charity (Phil. 4 : 10, 15, 16; 2 Cor.
11 : 8, 9) and seems organized.

Some organization is hinted at in the unusual salutation of Paul: " to the saints with the bishops and
deacons." While these words suggest the fact of organization, yet it is evidently recent, since Paul almost
forgets the " bishops and deacons " in his address: an
unmindfulness which makes it more than doubtful
that Paul had anything to do with their appointment.

It is the custom among high-churchmen of the
Anglican, and the Episcopal church in America, especially the latter, to assert that the Apostles fixed a
threefold order on the church. This procedure is ex-
plainable by the fact that their claims for their church
and their own official position depend upon this threefold order. But this is groundless supposition, contradicted by all the facts of early church history. There
is no discernible threefold order in the words of Paul
to the Romans (Ch. 12) nor in the gifts and ministrations of 1 Cor. 12.

The threefold order of servants of a church emerges
in the letters of Clement and the epistles of Ignatius.
The deacons, who have been a subsidiary order of
elders, acquire distinct position. As the deacons below, so the pastor-bishop above rises into distinction
from the other elders.

The Ignatian letters recognize (A. D. 150) in some
churches the existence of a *local* threefold order.
There is no diocesan bishop, no bishop of the Church

at large, only a local pastor-bishop. Of these there were thousands in the third century. When the Didache was written there was not yet a single ruling elder, but a presbytery. "Appoint for yourselves bishops and deacons" (XIV, 1, 2).

The later apostolic canons tell how a single pastor or bishop is to be elected. "If there are few men and not twelve persons" (an evident echo of the Twelve Apostles) "who are competent to vote at the election of a bishop, the neighbouring churches should be written to in order that three selected men may come to examine whether he is worthy." (See Lindsay, p. 178, note.)

Beside the pastor, the congregation was required to appoint at least two elders. (See Lindsay, p. 180.) Thus we have a presbyterial church, as the normal form, in the second and third century.

Of appointment or ordination by an apostle, or any successor of an apostle, there is not a word.

How the later bishop was evolved will next concern us.

XII

THE EVOLUTION OF EPISCOPACY AND PAPACY

The confusion of the first two centuries.

The suggestion : The name, bishop, evolved ; the office, devolved.

Under what other name was the " bishop " masquerading.

Was it, " deacon," or " elder " ?

The evolution of the name, bishop, indicates evolution of the office.

Episcopos is either superior deacon or elder.

Harnack's opinion. Hatch.

No threefold order in the primitive church.

Hatch quoted ; and Lightfoot.

The elements which demanded " government," Hatch.

The moment from which to date the Catholic church.

The bishop not successors of apostles, but of Christ.

The first appearance of apostolic, episcopal, succession.

The clerical class, and the influences producing it.

The consequences of the triumph of Christianity.

Catholic church authority and power.

Roman catholicism.

Papacy ; its evolution.

XII

THE EVOLUTION OF EPISCOPACY AND PAPACY

BISHOP GORE echoes a complaint that going backward after we leave the middle of the second century, we enter into a tunnel in which very little can be discerned. But, tunnels can be made by closing one's eyes ; darkness may be lack of vision. It is not that there is lack of light in the first two centuries that makes it hard to see clearly, but there is a confusion which reigns during that period. *This confusion is itself the best of arguments that The Church knew no successors to* the Apostles as having divine authority in The Church.

. The inability to discern clearly any one line of officers bearing apostolic authority has led to the suggestion that the contention is not concerning a name but a fact—that the *name, bishop, may have been e*volved, *but the office de*volved. This rather ingenious effort to dissociate the name from the office cannot be regarded as a success. If the diocesan bishop of the fourth century is not an evolution of the officer or servant who was called bishop in the first century, then he must have had during this period supremacy and apostolic authority *under some other name.* For, the supposition that the successor to the apostles, who for that reason would naturally be the superior in the church, was not recognized under some name, is hardly worth the making; so that those (like Canon Gore) who imagine the office *de*volved and the name *e*volved must tell us what name the supposed successor bore before he was called bishop and why the title, which he had borne for two or three centuries, was later changed to that of bishop.

The names by which the servants or officers in the early Church were known are apostles, prophets, teachers, angels, elders, episcopoi, deacons, governors, presidents, shepherds, evangelists, and the like. Under which one of these names was the successor of the apostles masquerading? To which one of these named officers, we have a right to demand, did the Apostles transmit supreme authority?

The choice must be made between the elder and the deacon. There is certainly no evidence that the apostles transmitted any supreme authority to the deacons, even though the earlier deacon may have later become the bishop, as some maintain. That an elder may have later been called, in an exclusive and special sense, bishop, we have seen to be the most probable. But, there is no evidence whatever that the *apostles* made either the deacon or the elder their successor. The idea that the " angel of the church " was successor to the apostles, is now abandoned.

The evolution of the *name*, bishop, is evidence of the evolution of the *office*, bishop. There was no officer *permanent* in *the* Church, nor in *a* church, to whom the name bishop was *later* given. The new name distinguished a new office. An elder, or possibly a deacon, was called a bishop because a new service needed a distinguishing name.   That new duties would appear in a growing society goes without saying, and that these new duties should give rise to new names, or to distinctive use of old names, is evident.

So the general name, episcopos, or overseer, agent, administrator, servant, became specific and designated either the superior deacon of the superior presbyter.

Harnack holds that the bishops were successors to the prophets and teachers and not to the apostles, who passed away earlier.   Hatch thinks that the name of the most esteemed function, that of oversight, epis-copein, would naturally be used to designate the single presbyter finally selected for this duty.

Thus *the name bishop came with an evolved, not a devolved, duty*, and the notion that the function was devolved from the apostles, as Gore and Moberly suggest, is found delusive.   It is the failure of a last resort.

As was said at the close of the last chapter the bishop is not first of a threefold order.   The threefold order : apostles, elders and deacons, was not established in any church.   In Jerusalem, James, not an apostle, was head of the church, even when Peter and John were there.   The " apostles and elders " form a kind of council or sanhedrin (see Acts 15 ; 6 : 22) which consults with the whole multitude.   There is no mention of deacons.   As we have seen the servants of Acts 6 are not so called and had no permanent office.

There was no office in the Jewish church corresponding to the later deacon. (See Hastings' Dictionary, s. v.)

The threefold order first appears in the time of
Ignatius (c. 150 A. D.). From such of his letters as
are original it is evident that the church in his day was
a precise type of the modern local presbyterian
church, having a pastor, or bishop, elders and deacons.
Experience evolved this order. In Paul's day there
was no such fixed order, and even in the time of Ignatius it was not universal.

As the pastor, or bishop, in a single congregation
came to eminence by a natural process, so did the
diocesan bishop secure eminence among local bishops.

" Between the primitive episcopos and the mediæval
bishop there is so wide an interval that those who are
familiar with the picture of the latter may find it
difficult to recognize the portrait of the former. At
the same time, that interval is not the chasm of an
impassable gulf, it is a space of discernible ground
every step of which can be traced " (Hatch, p. 107).

Some time in the second century most, if not all, of
the Christian churches had a single pastor or bishop
at its head, with a body of elders, *i. e.*, presbyters and
deacons, as his assistants. How early is disputed.
Lightfoot says that about the middle of the second
century each church or organized Christian community had its bishop (or pastor), presbyters and
deacons.

In A. D. 170 Dionysius of Corinth is first intrusted
with the bishopric of that city. We learn from
Eutychius that as late as 188 A. D. there were no
bishops in the whole of provincial Egypt. (See
Brown, p. 200.)

It is not necessary to assume, and there is no evidence warranting any other than what we may call natural causes producing the transition. In writing to the Corinthian church, Paul reminds them that "nature" teaches some things. Common sense calls for a presiding mind and hand in a church.

Dr. Hatch has named the natural elements which entered into the formation of church government. These were:

(1) The management of the finances including the charitable funds, (2) the conduct of the religious services, (3) the celebration of the communion and love feasts, (4) the teaching function of a church, (5) the determination of what was true apostolic doctrine, (6) the maintenance of unity and peace in the Christian community, (7) the exercise of discipline, (8) the reception of members and the reinstatement of the lapsed.

The solution of these problems evolved, by a kind of necessity, the episcopate. Hatch (p. 38) says, and it expresses the exact truth, "the episcopate grew by force of circumstances."

In those days a monarchical episcopate was almost a necessity, therefore it came into being. The state of society called for it.

One of the most important steps was the decision that only one bishop should be in a community of Christians however large. This was the outcome of the dispute between Novatian and Cyprian. Novatian was head of the puritan party in Rome. He was elected Bishop of Rome by this party after the election by the anti-puritans of a bishop. It was a valid election. To overthrow him the new principle was announced, that *Rome already possessed ecclesiastical organization.*

This is the moment from which we may date the Roman Catholic church.

Cyprian of Africa used his great influence for this principle, to have the election of Novatian declared null. In the interest of unity, any one who claimed to be a member of the Christian Church must belong to the one organization of the city or community. The attempt to form two churches side by side was a schism. *This is the first decisive step* in the formation of the Episcopal, and later, of the Roman Catholic church.

It is decisive against the apostolic succession of the bishops that the early theory was, *not that bishops succeeded the apostles, but that the bishop in the church represented Christ, the absent Lord, and the presbyters were in the place of the apostles.*

The theory of apostolic succession appears in the third century, that as the bishops preserve the apostolic teaching, they must be also successors to the apostles.

The view that bishops and not presbyters are the successors of the apostles appears first, says Hatch (p. 105) by implication in the claim of Zephrinius and Callistus during the Montanist controversy. Probably the earliest express statement is by an African bishop about the same time (A. D. 250).

Then came the claim for the bishop of the power of " binding and loosing." Tertullian protested against it. This did not gain general acceptance until the fifth century.

It was a still later development of apostolic succession that the bishop also succeeded to the assumed power of the apostles in the conferring of spiritual gifts and that through them exclusively the Holy Spirit entered into souls in baptism and into church officers at ordination. This was received as a doctrine by the council of Paris (A. D. 829) (Hatch, pp. 106-7).

The creation of a superior or clerical class was the gradual work of causes plainly discernible. Hatch gives the evidence that originally laymen could not only teach and baptize but also celebrate the Eucharist.

He and other writers maintain that Montanism was the reaction of the old spirit in the church against what became later monarchism. Spiritual gifts had precedence in the early church. In the later church, organization was more important.

The influences which produced a clerical caste, briefly summarized were these:

(1) The growing corruption in the church and the lowering of the standard of membership.

(2) The intense desire for order, which was generated by the decay of the empire.

(3) The growing belief that the Christian ministry had succeeded to the Jewish or the Levitical priesthood.

Bishops came, says Brown, not as Hatch says, upon financial considerations, nor as Ramsay on basis of intercommunication but by the cessation of charis-

matic gifts among the general body of believers
(pp. 219–221).

The fourth century witnessed marvellous changes.
From a persecuted sect, Christianity became the national religion, and heresy was a crime punishable by
law.

The state became the forceful arm of the catholic
church. It was of interest to the civil rulers that there
be but one church. Hence it gave its authority and
power to aid in securing this result. During the earlier
centuries a majority had no means of coercing a
minority.

The decree of the church at Jerusalem had been but
a request, a dogma, and not a command. Later, the
decrees of councils are like the edicts of the Empire.
Constantine was the chief agent in the erection of the
catholic church from without. A law of Constantine,
A. D. 326, confines the privileges and immunities
granted to Christians to those observing catholic law.
When the ordination of Cæcilian threatened to divide
the African churches, Constantine summoned all the
bishops of Christendom to a council at Arles. Those
taking part in the council were bound by its decisions. Thus Christian churches surrendered their
independence and became parts of the one catholic
church. The linking together of all the churches of
the empire gave immense effect to any decisions.
Thenceforth excommunication was a terrible power
and terribly abused. This magnificent organization
thus developed, the catholic church has long outlived
the power of the state which was its outward creator.

Yet it was not complete in the sense of embracing all Christian communities. There were those who were called the autokephaloi. " They were in the position which Cyprian had in earlier times asserted to be the true position of all bishops: their responsibility was to God alone" (Hatch, p. 181).

There was perfect truth in the statement of the Donatists that this catholic church was " a geographical expression." It was not a union of Christians effected by God's spirit, but effected by state power. The Donatists were crushed by the state. The secular power made ecclesiastical puritanism a crime.

This is, hastily sketched, the rise, growth, and usurpation of the episcopacy. It was meant for good. It accomplished good. Its alliance with state power corrupted it with arrogance and wealth. It is not apostolic either as to the succession of its bishops, nor in the spirit of its authority, nor in the doctrine which it came to teach. It gave birth to a church which could not really conquer the world, but for nearly a thousand years was conquered by the welt geist, " the god of this world."

The Roman Catholic church is the most powerful form of the evolution of the catholic concept of The Church.

The supremacy of the Roman bishop began to be actual in the fourth century. At the Council of Sardica (A. D. 347) there was given the Bishop of Rome appellate jurisdiction. This decision, that appeals *might* be made to Rome, proves that it was not theretofore either law or custom. It was the Emperor

Theodosius who, in 380 A. D., published a law in which
he commanded that those who followed that law take
the name of " Catholic Christians " ; of others it was
declared " their meetings shall not have the name of
churches." This was a beginning. At this time
supremacy was not conceded by all the bishops to
Rome. It was an *imperial* fact, rather than a religious
fact. It was a novelty, and was effected by state authority in the interest of political unity which seemed
to require religious conformity.

Both St. Basil and St. Jerome denied any supremacy
to the pope. Jerome says, " let the ambition of Roman
preëminence retire. I speak to the successor of the
fisherman and the disciple of the Cross." The œcumenical council at Constantinople (381 A. D.) decreed
that no bishop should invade the diocese of another
bishop. " The bishop of Alexandria shall manage the
affairs of Egypt alone, and the bishops of the East
preside over the East alone." (See Hussey, p. 23 f.)
It was in contradiction to this decree, which earlier
popes said should abide to the end of the world, that
the papacy became more assuming and assertive.

The supremacy of the Roman bishop over the western church was as much of a usurpation as the domination of the Empire had been, and like it, also, was
largely secured through force, intrigue and forgeries.
(See Hussey, p. 51 ff.) Thus, in the well-known case
of Apiarius, Bishop of Sicca, Pope Zosimus used a fal-
sified version of the Nicene canons which the African
Synod repudiated. This Synod (422 A. D.), requested
the Pope, in almost so many words, to mind his own

business, that he shall not send any more nuncios to interfere with them in any business *for fear the church should suffer through pride and ambition* (Hussey, p. 47), a fear abundantly, terribly realized.

The Council of Chalcedon (451 A. D.), pronounced against the claims of the pope to universal sovereignty, by giving the See of Constantinople equal rank to that of Rome. But this did not hinder the assumption of supremacy by the popes.

The Pope Gelasius was the first to set the authority of the papacy above that of the state (492 A. D.). He says to the Emperor Anastasius that two powers govern the world, the sacred authority of the pontiffs and the royal power. He gives reasons why the priest is superior to the king.

Another step in this progress was marked (507 A. D.) when Ennodius declared that St. Peter bequeathed his own merits to his successors as well as his authority. " For who can doubt the sanctity of one raised to such a height of dignity; in whom, if there is a lack of goodness acquired by his own merits, that which his predecessors bestow is enough." Surely the Apostle Peter must have had an inexhaustible supply of sanctity to make holy many of the popes, of some of whom even the catholic historian Möhler says, " Hell has swallowed them up " (Symbolik, p. 353; Foster, p. 22).

But to follow all the steps is needless. Popery is a growth,—one pretension added to another in a disordered and demoralized condition of society when might was right. Each pope went a little beyond his pred-

ecessor until finally the Pope Pius IX is declared infallible. Temporal power reached its climax in Gregory
VII and Innocent III. The nineteenth century has
seen the popes shorn of such power, yet the claim is
still maintained.

The Fourth Lateran (general) Council decided that
" if any temporal power shall have neglected to purge
his dominions of heresy—he, the pope, may declare his
subjects absolved from their allegiance," etc. (Hussey,
p. 40). The papacy will rule alone—when it can.
Innocent III has thus described a pope: " The vicar
of Jesus Christ, the successor of Peter, the anointed of
the Lord, the God of Pharaoh, short of God, beyond
man, less than God, greater than man, who judges all
men and is judged by no man " (Hussey, p. 199).

Thus the catholic idea evolved. This is its outcome.

How far removed from its humble origin, how very
different, Loisy has frankly admitted. The Papacy,
in attempting to absorb the elements of the world,
has become mundane.

XIII

GENERAL ARGUMENTS OF GORE AND MOBERL

The admitted failure of historical argument.
The "should be" argument.
Ananias' act in Paul's ordination, invalid.
The exclusion of non-catholic from the covenant.
The Holy Spirit confined to apostolic succession.
Lightfoot criticised by Gore and Moberly.
Ministerial character from above.
What is "from above."
The "home of grace and truth."
"Catholicism" no base of union.
Have catholics more grace than protestants?
The moral gains of apostolic succession.
Anxiety about succession.
Ideals of the ministry.
The "catholic" church as channel of grace.
Corporate Christianity, and "lapsing."
Were Savonarola, George Fox, the Wesleys, failures?
The need of "organs" and the body.
The Spirit not operative exclusively on the clergy.
Church and Kingdom.

XIII

GENERAL ARGUMENTS OF GORE AND MOBERLY

In default of historical arguments which might establish the catholic concept, that The Church is an organized entity, with some divinely determined authority, it is not uncommon for its defenders to fall back on general principles, *a priori* considerations, which make it reasonable to suppose that there *should have been, therefore there was*, a catholic church originally. So Bishop Gore and Canon Moberly argue. The failure of the historical argument is admitted by Gore who says (p. 337): "There has been apostolic succession from the *latter part of the second century.*" Moberly (p. 116) puts it, without sufficient warrant, as far back as Clement, as a *principle implanted in the consciousness* of The Church. Since this historical bridge which the catholic constructs fails to reach the other side of the chasm, the gap is filled in by both Gore and Moberly and other catholic writers, by suppositions, and arguments that are generalizations from suppositions. For example, Gore says (p. 222): "It was Christ's *intention* that there should be this stewardship" in the apostolic succession. Gore speaks of the "ordination which *we should suppose* Apollos to have received" (p. 249). In Diotrephes "we should *probably* be inclined to see one of these local bishops"

187

(p. 255). "We should *suppose* bishops always existed in so prominent a church as Rome. If not in name, *we can well believe* there was an episcopal succession from the first." [Italics our own.]

Very much of the reasoning of these able writers is specious, though honestly intended.

It is not correct to say (Gore, p. 10), "Christ instituted a society for men to belong to *as a means* of belonging to Him." Of course there is some truth in this, yet, more correctly, the reverse is the case: those belonging to Christ form The Church. It is an unwarranted assumption, contradicted by the New Testament, as by the Old Testament, and subsequent facts, that "spiritual gifts are given by sacraments" and that "thus the Christian's spiritual privileges depend on his membership of a visible society" (Gore, p. 57). It is not to be denied that there are blessings for the individual Christian inseparable from his being in association with other Christians, and sacraments are useful. But do facts affirm that *only these who belong to a so-called "catholic" church have "spiritual privileges," "spiritual gifts"* ?

Gore again says (p. 70): "No ministerial act could be regarded as valid, unless it was performed under the shelter of a commission received by the transmission of authority delegated by Christ Himself *to His Apostles*." Then Ananias' act was invalid when he laid hands on Saul (Paul) and he received his sight; then the sending forth of Barnabas and Paul by the unknown prophets of Antioch was invalid; all the ministerial acts of all except the few who claim (*it is only a claim*, which any society can make) apostolic succession are invalid. This is to contradict, we must say, God Himself, who has made valid—who can doubt it?—the ministrations of such men as Luther and Calvin and Wesley. Yet Dr. Gore does not hesitate to declare the ministry of the "various Presbyterian and Congregational organizations invalid, that is, it falls outside the conditions of covenanted security" (p. 345). Well may Canon Bruce (p. 126) exclaim: "A tremendous statement, a sentence of excommunication, of exclusion from the covenant of grace and life of a hundred million Christians."

This is surely a case when the words apply : " Call not thou that common and unclean which God has cleansed." That ministry is not to be called invalid which God has blessed to the redemption of mankind. This comes close to ascribing to Beelzebub the work of the Holy Spirit.

How strange the inquiry sounds, " Could any Christian receive the gift of the Holy Spirit except by the laying on of apostolic hands?" (Gore, p. 357), with the implication that only through apostolic succession comes the gift of the Holy Spirit. It seems to imply blindness to great facts to ask: "Was there ever a time in church history when men who deserted the authoritative ministry and set up one of their own outside the due succession, would have been regarded as still within the covenant?" Regarded by whom as within the covenant? Did not God regard Luther and Calvin and Cranmer and Ridley and Wesley as

within the covenant? Are not the ministers of the
Reformed Episcopal church or the old Catholic within
the covenant? Has not Bishop Gore himself deserted
the "authoritative ministry of the Roman Catholic
church from which the Anglican came out"?

Gore inquires (p. 357): "Was it ever a recognized
principle in the Church that an unordained Christian
could celebrate the Eucharist?" To this inquiry
Hatch has amply replied, and any one versed in the
history of Christian institutions may readily reply,
that the Eucharist, that is, the Lord's Supper, was
celebrated without any priest, by laymen and prophets,
in the early Church.

It is altogether misleading to suppose that a re-
organization of Christians in some new form of church
government and service is a recreation of The Church.
It is therefore superfluous to say, as Dr. Gore takes the
trouble to do, that "the Church was not created by
man, nor can it be recreated from time, in view of
varying circumstances." Yet, is not this a valid
criticism the Roman Catholic makes as to the Anglican church?

Both Canon Gore and Canon Moberly find it necessary to charge Bishop Lightfoot with great oversight.
Gore says of Lightfoot's essay on the Christian Ministry: "Strangely enough the question is never faced,
did Christ institute a ministry in the person of His
Apostles, and did they perpetuate it?" And Moberly
says: "Must true ministerial character be, in all
cases, conferred from above, or may it be evolved
from below? Is uninterrupted transmission really

essential?" He says, as to this question, " Lightfoot
never answers it, never raised it, it never presents
itself to his mind" (p. 116).

The fact is, Lightfoot answers it so conclusively that
the advocate of apostolic succession would fain ignore
his answer by charging him with an oversight of the
very matter he is dealing with, from the beginning to
the end of his essay.

What, we must inquire, do these magical words
" from above" and " from below" mean? Does a
king occupy his seat "from above" and a president
" from below"? Is not a ministry like that of the
prophets in the first Christian century, from above?
Was not Paul's ministry from above? Was David
Livingstone's ministry from below? Is not the ministry of William Booth from above? Or is it from
below?

It seems hard for the advocate of apostolic succession to understand that "from above" is from the
Spirit of God, and that the Spirit may use any humble
instrument to effect His call. A John may baptize a
Jesus; an Ananias may lay hands on a Paul, and unknown prophets ordain the first Christian missionary
apostles, at Antioch.

The catholic notion cannot be defended on the supposition that Jesus instituted " a society to be the
home of the grace and truth which He came to bring,"
as Gore says.

Certainly the catholic church, like Israel of old, has
not proved to be any such " home of grace and truth."
It is true enough that the catholic church " claims to

have been instituted as the home of the new covenant
of salvation" (Gore, p. 11). So Israel still claims to
be the home of the old covenant of salvation, and why
is not that as true? There is no " home" for grace
and truth except the " heart of man," and that may
be no home. No institution can house grace and
truth. Nor does it prove anything to say: " He—
Jesus—would not have cast them abroad among men,
but would have given them a stable home" (p. 12).
Israel, God's chosen people, rejected the grace and
truth which came by Jesus. Why must the " catholic"
church be a more perfect home than ancient Israel?

Canon Gore is on dangerous ground when he argues
for apostolic succession because it serves as a bond of
union. On the contrary, it has often served as a di-
viding wedge. Has it preserved unity among the
churches which, as Gore concedes, have this succession?
What delightful harmony between the Greek and the
Roman and the Anglican churches, not to speak of
the Nestorian and the other Oriental churches, which
have this means of preserving unity and truth and the
transmission of divine grace!

It is even more dangerous when he says of its sec-
ond important use (p. 77), " that it impresses upon
Christians that their new life is a communicated gift."
Has it so done?

Who most regards his spiritual life as a gift from
God—a Quaker, like George Fox, or the sacramenta-
rian? Do catholics, as a class, really depend more
than non-catholics " upon grace given from above "?

Go to any non-protestant country and behold how

effectively this theory has stopped men from looking to God, has kept them looking to the church, the priest and the bishop.

The " sacraments are covenanted channels of grace " if these be faithfully and spiritually received. But, when Gore, seeking support from Irenæus (contrary to Lightfoot's understanding of his teaching), says that there is actual fleshly partaking of Christ, then he is contradicted by his own book of prayer which makes the communion effective only when worthily received.

To teach " men to worship God under the form of bread," as a high-church Anglican has declared to be desirable (Lee), is not the way of worshipping God in spirit and in truth.

Gore says (p. 81) : " Apostolic succession seems to correspond, as nothing else does, to the moral needs of the ministry of Christ's church."

Here, we really reach the root of the whole matter of apostolic succession. It is nothing else than the very human and very weak desire for pedigree.

That there comes advantage with ancient origin and a long line of ancestors and lineage that goes back into obscurity, we may admit. But it is an advantage simply because it imposes upon those who have not the ability to discern real merit, and it is a gain chiefly to such only as have not power in and of themselves.

Yet, Moberly also (page 123) urges this, that " each minister is anxious about his ordination, about his pedigree," and he says, in default of actual proof of apostolic succession, that " each generation may be expected to look after its own descent."

This notion is unsupported by facts. Thousands of Methodists and Lutherans and Presbyterians and other protestant ministers do not, to-day, worry about their succession.

How strongly this idea is impressed on the high churchmen, is seen also when Bishop Satterlee writes: " Those who are outwardly consecrated by an authority, which is derived by a chain of outward, visible, historical acts, directly from the apostles" (which of course is Satterlee's unprovable assumption, denied by the leading divines of the Anglican church) " *have a much higher ideal* of that ministry than would be possible had they been merely admitted to it by ordinances which the church had originated for itself in post-apostolic times."

If this means that the Anglican and Roman priests have a higher ideal than *they* would have had without a belief in such descent, we will leave to those priests to say. But, if he means to imply that those having this fancied connection have higher ideals than ministers in other churches who cannot accept claims disproved by history, then Bishop Satterlee is contradicted by the facts ; because, it is manifestly untrue that Methodists, and Baptists, and Lutherans, and Presbyterians, and other evangelical ministers, are below the priests of the Anglican, or the Roman, or the Greek, or the Eastern catholic churches, in their ideals, and in living up to those ideals.

The mere names of Luther, and Calvin, and Knox, and George Fox, and Wesley and Edwards, and Eliot, and thousands of others who might be mentioned, suffice to refute this assumption that apostolic succession meets the moral need of the ministry.

As a matter of fact, the priest often wants authority because of a sense of weakness as to spiritual power, and because he desires the support of an authority which, not having it in his message nor in himself, he seeks to derive from an institution.

It must be regarded as a singular fact, according to the high church notion, that God, having prepared a channel through which to pour His divine grace into the hearts and lives of men, has seen fit, in such large measure, to abandon that channel, and to employ others entirely without it.

Moberly argues that The Church was corporate (by which he means, definitely organized) because membership was essential to being a Christian, and this required a body to belong to. He says, after quoting certain passages from the Epistles: " If lapsing from effective membership was *ipso facto* Christian failure, this shows that the requirements of corporate Christianity were from the first irksome to the flesh and that the necessary coherence of the church was from the first an indispensable element in the Christian ideal" (p. 12). If corporate Christianity meant nothing else than an episcopal society, then we do not wonder that some found it irksome at the first, as many since have. But, was not the secession of the Anglican church a lapse from the " corporate Christianity " of the Roman Catholic church, of which it had been before a part? Does the mere fact that bishops ordained in and by the Roman church took part in this schism render it any the less so? Does not the Episcopal church in America regard the " Reformed Episcopal Church " as a schism?

Yet bishops took part in this schism.

It cannot be considered a fact that " lapsing from membership " was " ipso facto Christian failure." Are millions of protestants to be regarded as " *ipso facto* Christian failures " because they refuse to share in what seem to them the errors of some representative of " corporate Christianity "?

Fellowship with other Christians was *not* " irksome at the first." Here and there some withdrew from this fellowship, but it was not from corporate Christianity. Paul did not preach corporate Christianity. When he urged unity on the church at Corinth, it was a unity of feeling, thought, action. It was the authority of the Spirit they were to yield to. They should be one in Christ Jesus, not in an episcopal society.

Canon Moberly argues that Christ must have given The Church a ministry because the body needs organs. What Christ theoretically should have done is not in question. We are dealing with facts, not theory. But the theory is incorrect, as Moberly presents it. He says, the body cannot exist without " organs." This is not correct as a physiological fact. " Organs " in the sense of the word as Moberly uses it, are not necessary to the existence of the body, though they are to its *best* existence; unless by " organs " he means the heart or lungs and other internal functional centres. But he does not mean this, for he talks only of the eye and ear and hand. He says the

body does not confer on these organic power, and concludes that therefore The Church as a body cannot
confer power on its ministers. But there is a very
real sense in which the body does confer on the organ
its functional power.

And *the one organ in the body cannot possibly confer the functional power to another* organ, as Gore and
Moberly expect one leading organ, the bishop, to confer power on other organs, the priest and deacon. In
the human body no one organ depends directly upon
another. The analogy is fatal to the " high " church
theory. The rejection of a bodily organ lies within
the body's power. So Christ said: if thine eye
offend, pluck it out; if thine hand offend, cut it off.
Or, translated into the analogy of Gore and Moberly,
if thy bishop offend thee, cast him away ; if thy priest,
cut him off. This was what the reformed church did
at the Reformation.

The body is absolutely dependent on no external
organ for its vitality ; nor does The Church depend on
a bishop or on many bishops.

Another difficulty with this theory as Gore puts it
(p. 71) is that he makes *the ministry*, the apostolic
succession, *that which is " assumed by the Spirit from
above."* That is, we have *a virtual denial that the
Church is the body of Christ.* It is the ministry
which, Gore says, like Christ's body, is caught up by
the Spirit.

When Moberly says that Christ announced His
Church first under the name of Kingdom, he is far
from the true understanding of either Church or

Kingdom. As Hort says, " the identity of these two, common since St. Augustine's day, must be abandoned. The church is the ' visible representation ' of the kingdom."

In Christ's teaching the Kingdom and Church are not the same, as any one can test by reading the Gospels and putting the word church for kingdom. " The *Church* is at hand." " Blessed are the poor in spirit, for theirs is the *Church*."

But even if it were so that Christ first announced the Church in terms of the Kingdom, this would not prove that the Church was an organized society, since the Kingdom is not present in any organic sense. The Kingdom of God, in New Testament teaching, is certainly invisible. It cometh not with observation. It is hidden as seed or leaven. To Augustine the Kingdom of the Church was as real and as organic as the Roman Empire. And he, with his contemporaries, sought to substitute the one city for the other. And this conception of the church prevailed for a thousand years. But, it is a total misconception which has wrought frightful evils.

It does not stand any better with Moberly's attempt to argue the organic visibility of the Church because it is the body of Christ. Manifestly, The Church is the body of Christ only in a figurative sense. Christ had only one body. We speak of the " body politic," by which we mean an organization the members of which are politically one. Christians are one body because they are spiritually one. May not any number of men acquire visibility as a society and unity simply by swearing a common oath of allegiance to themselves or to some idea? Their organic visibility is not dependent on any form of organization, but a unity of purpose which from within makes them one. The strongest unity obtainable among men is that which comes not from common laws and customs, but inward love. And even if such rites as baptism and communion were as necessary as they are expedient, yet these do not depend upon a set ministry any more than a family feast depends upon a priest.

XIV

THE MARKS OF THE CHURCH

Cardinal Gibbons' "marks."
The Creed of A. D. 381.
How ascertain the true marks.
Jesus Christ presents the marks.
The "catholic" marks found among "Masons."

1. The *Unity* of the Church.

Outward unity easily secured.
The "catholic" means for securing unity.
The many schisms in catholic churches.
Anathematize all who differ.
Horrors of the papacy.
Antagonism of Roman, Greek, Anglican.
Inability of catholics to unite.

2. *Catholicity*.

The claim of mere extension.
The Roman definition.
Vincent's dictum.
No one church, as organized, catholic.
All belonging to Christ in the Catholic Church.

3. *Sanctity*.

Are the catholic churches *holy*?
New Testament "saints."
The worship of catholic churches not holy.

found. Are we involved in a vicious circle of reasoning? Are we to conclude concerning The Church
from our concept of it, or are we to derive our concept from our knowledge of The Church? Shall we
detect The Church by marks, or deduce the marks
from The Church? The Church must exist concretely
before one can form any abstract notion as to The
Church. The Church is not a bundle of notions.
The Church is the name given to an historical fact.
There was something to which the name "Ecclesia"
was given. Our notion of the marks of this thing
must be derived from the thing itself. When and
only when we know the historical Church, can we
affirm such and such are its marks.

What are the marks of a man? Unless I have a
perception of man I can form no concept of him.
What are the marks of a state? Unless I have a perception of a state I cannot say what its marks are.
We distinguish between what is essential to the man,
or the state, and what is accidental. I see that the
colour of a man's skin, his size, etc., are not essential.
I see that a state may be aristocratic, autocratic or
democratic, and that these do not affect its being. I
would be guilty of the same bad logic of which the
catholic is guilty, who says that a church must be
episcopal, if I were to say, a state must be monarchical,
or a man must be white or black. I do, indeed, perceive that certain animals may and must be classed
together, and called for convenience, man.

I perceive that certain associations of men must be
classified, as family, or state. So I perceive that oth-

ers have a distinct raison d'être, namely: the maintenance and performance of religious life and service in
a fashion which has its origin in Jesus Christ. These
associations I must call churches, because they correspond with a recognizable percept, a body of men
associated together by means of the Spirit of Jesus
Christ and to perpetuate His life and work. To say
that these men must associate all in one mode or
fashion is like saying that all governments must be
republican.

It may be that *a* church has other marks than those
which characterize *The* Church, *e. g.*, episcopacy or
presbytery, immersion or celibacy. There is no correct way of forming an abstract notion of what The
Church ought to be apart from the knowledge of The
Church. Have we a percept of The Church? Surely,
we have it in the person of Jesus Christ Himself who
is The Church; we have it less clearly perhaps, yet
discernibly, in the disciples whom He gathered about
Himself and to whom He gave communion. The
Church, we perceive in the company of those who believed that Jesus was the Christ, the Mediator of the
New Covenant and who more and more gave him
supremacy in their lives, and multiplied His influence
in others who were brought to acknowledge that
Jesus was the Christ, Mediator and Redeemer. To
ascertain what the marks of The Church are, we should
first study Him who was, historically, the new fountain and source of Church life. As we have seen there
is a very real sense in which The Church did not
originate with Christ, so far as it means the company

of God's righteous ones. But, it is essentially true that Jesus Christ presents The Church ideally as well as really. The Church must bear, as Paul says of himself, " the marks of Jesus Christ." No one thinks of doubting that the Church is the body of Jesus Christ. But, a man's body is the abode and manifestation form of the life which *is* the man. The marks of Christ's *Church* must be, of course, the marks of that visible *Christ* which was among men as a flesh-body.

The marks of Jesus Christ were the signs which witnessed that the Spirit of God was in Him. It characterized Jesus as Christ, that He lived through the Spirit for God and man, that He mediated God's grace and favour to man, and man's service and love towards God.

Despite the frequent misconception of the words, we may say, that He did the work of prophet, priest and king. These words express in different form what —without here going with thoroughness into the question—was Christ's mission : to bring man to God, and God to man, which is the reconciliation or atonement. For this He was equipped. " How say ye of Him whom the Father hath sanctified and sent into the world, thou blasphemest" (John 10 : 36). And it is again written : " for Him hath God the Father sealed." So He said : " As My Father hath sent Me, even so send I you."

Therefore The Church, as Christ's body, can be recognized by the marks which make it evident that any body of men has the Spirit of Christ and is doing Christ's work in the world. This and this alone marks the true Church. The marks of *a*, and of *The*, True Church, are the marks of Jesus Christ, a spiritual worship of God and a loving service of man to the end that God and man are brought together, made one. Therefore the marks which the catholic churches, which are named Greek, or the Roman, or otherwise, emphasize: unity, sanctity, catholicity, apostolicity, must be carefully understood before one can assent that these are the marks of The Church.

A moment's reflection shows that some of these might characterize such a society as the Masons, for example. There is a unity about the Masons, which the Roman Catholic church does not surpass, and hardly equals. When Cardinal Gibbons boasts that his church has the same religious services all the world over, he can say no more than any Mason can say. When the Cardinal boasts that his church spreads over all the world, so are Masons found everywhere. Masons claim a measure of sanctity, which certainly the catholic has not always exceeded, so far as sanctity and morality or brotherly kindness are one. If the Masons do not claim apostolicity, they claim very ancient origin, and their claim is as reasonable as that Peter and Paul founded the church at Rome, or transmitted to it any authority. Unity and sanctity and universality and an ancient origin may characterize other bodies than a church. We cannot recognize The Church by these even though these characterize it. How marvelous that these " plain marks " are evident only to those who claim them for their own particular church.

1. Unity of the Church

That there must be a unity about any one thing, it
is almost as ridiculous to affirm, as it is absurd to deny.
What have we gained when we say The Church is
One? "I believe in One Holy Catholic Church,"—
certainly not in two. *Any* church must be *one* church.
This is as true of the "Dowie" society or the
Mormons, until a schism takes place, as of Baptists,
Methodists, or Catholics. That *a* church is *one* cannot
be any evidence or mark that it is *the* Church, because
all churches can claim unity, and have unity. For
example, the Samaritans form one church. We do
not, as evangelicals, confess that The Church *is* one,
so much as that there is *but one* Church, however
divided it appear, among men, on the surface. The
only sense in which we can affirm that the Church is
one, is that essential oneness of the Spirit of Christ
which binds all Christians together in a oneness which
God sees, even if man does not see it. The unity
which is sometimes claimed by and for the catholic,
whether called Greek, Roman or Anglican, is not a
unity which corresponds with the New Testament
notion, nor has it ever been secured within even the
narrow limits of an ecclesiastical organization by
Christlike means, nor has it contributed to the visible
unity of The Church. The boasted unity of the
Roman Catholic church is a unity which has been
secured by means diametrically opposed to the spiritual means by which alone true Church unity can
become and continue fact. It has been secured by
anathemas and excommunications. As Cardinal Gib-

bon says ("Church of Our Fathers"), "Should a catholic contumaciously deny a single article of faith he ceases to be a member of the church and is cut off as a withered branch."

By the process of declaring all Christians who are not subservient to the papacy to be without The Church, the Roman church maintains its unity despite the fact that there exist other churches equally ancient and in every sense that it claims for itself equally catholic, such are the Orthodox (Greek) church, and the other Oriental churches. Yet all these churches maintain this absurd claim of unity each against the other, and some even claiming this mark of unity for the Anglican church. The doctrine of the papacy is: "There is no church except that which is under the papal government," and this is what the Roman Catholic calls "the mark of unity," ignoring or denying the name of Church to millions of Christians!

Despite this doctrine, however, this same unity has been broken by no less than thirty schisms in the millennium from 500 to 1500 A. D.

The dominant faction in these schismatic struggles is always *the Church* which preserves this blessed unity. The unsuccessful faction is always "no church" and is anathematized. So the Greek church and the Anglican and all other non-Roman churches are not churches in the Roman Catholic sense.

Has all reason forsaken men, that they should call such unity a mark of Christ's body? Which was pope, Silverius or Vigilius? Formosus or Stephen?

Benedict, Sylvester, John or Gregory? The uncertainty as to the popes is made emphatic by the official announcement of the Pontifical Annual in the last year of Pius X, that the number of popes was 258, not 263. Five supposed popes of this " one " church pass into nonentity!

This fiction of unity has led to the commission by every catholic church which maintains it, of many crimes against man and sins against God. This unity must be maintained by the destruction of all who deny it. In order that it might be the *one* church, the Roman Catholic church has sinned above all others. Because it was the *only* church, no one could be saved without its fold.

" The unity of the ecclesiastical body is of so much importance, that only to those who remain in it are the ecclesiastical sacraments profitable, and no one, even if he shall have shed his blood for the name of Christ, can be saved except he shall have remained in the bosom and unity of the ' catholic ' church." So says a papal bull.

And the " Bull " of Boniface VIII (A. D. 1302), called *unam sanctam*, says: " None who are not found in the Catholic Church can become partakers of eternal life, but shall go into eternal fire which is prepared for the devil and his angels, except they shall have been gathered into the same before the end of life." " Moreover we declare, say, define and pronounce that it is altogether necessary to the salvation of every human creature to be subject to the Roman pontiff."

This doctrine has been repeatedly enunciated by the

Roman Catholic church. As late as 1847 Pope Pius IX declared: " Let, therefore, those who wish to be saved come to the pillar and ground of the truth, which is the church." And the Syllabus of 1864 condemns the error that there is a well founded hope for the eternal salvation of those who are in no manner in the true church.

The Vatican council (1870) anathematizes all those who " presume to contradict" the definition of the papal infallibility. In its enforcement of this conviction—and we shall not here dispute that some held it honestly,—the Roman Catholic church has acted with merciless consistency. Some deceived themselves that they were really acting in the interest of soul-salvation. Many, however, made this a pretext and a cover, for ambition and cruelty. Wars, insurrections, persecutions and cruelties such as no other human power has ever been guilty of, were caused by such Popes as Gregory VII, Innocent III, Innocent IV, Martin IV, and many others. The crusade,—what a name!—against the Albigenses has probably no parallel for inhuman cruelty and nameless outrages perpetrated by those to whom Heaven was promised by the papal authority for their successful prosecution of the purposes of the papacy. We would not allude in even this passing way to these horrible scenes, if it were not necessary to briefly suggest the undeniable fact that the means whereby the Roman Catholic church sought to maintain its unity and make itself the one and " catholic " church were such as exceed in inhumanity those ever employed by any secular

power, and this not for a brief episode, but for centuries. The march of Mohammedanism was peace
itself compared with the course of the papacy from the
fifth to the fifteenth century.

And, be it especially noted, it was the false concept of The Church and its unity which gave seeming
excuse and palliation to these excesses.

The oneness of the Orthodox (Greek) church is like
that of Rome: maintained by force, secured by exclusion of those who differ, and continued by refusals to
unite with other Christians. It has refused, on no sufficient grounds, as determined by Scripture standards, all
union and fellowship with other Christian churches.

As late as A. D. 1439 attempts at union with the
Roman Catholics were made and nearly consummated,
but the Patriarch of the East in a synod at Jerusalem
condemned those who had any part in the proceed-
ings.

Melancthon sought union between the Lutherans
and the Greeks, and efforts were later made (A. D.
1572–1594) for several years on the part of the
Lutherans in this direction, but they were repulsed
by the ignorant and unfortunate Patriarch of Constantinople.

The Anglican church made advances in 1862, but
the Greek church refused to recognize Anglican
baptism, expressed serious scruples about the validity
of Anglican orders and condemned the second marriage
of many of their bishops and priests. They insisted
on the rejection of the "filioque" clause, on the
veneration of the icons, trine immersion and the

transformation of the elements in the Eucharist. All the Greek church conceded to the Anglican church was the pitiful permission to bury their dead in consecrated ground, without, however, owning a foot of it (Schaff, "Creeds," 1 : 75).

The part of the church of which the œcumenical Patriarch at Constantinople is head recently (1903) addressed an appeal to the Holy Synod (Russian) looking towards better relations with Roman Catholics and Protestant churches.

The Holy Synod replied : " In reference to our relation with the Roman Catholic and Protestant churches it can only be repeated that the Holy Synod will in the future as in the past, pray that these branches of Christendom may be reunited to the original church, for the Orthodox church is the one catholic and apostolic church from which the others in their errors have departed."

" The only part of Western Christendom with which a closer communion seems possible is the ritualistic breach of the Anglican church, although here too the influence of Calvinism is still too strong."

2.   CATHOLICITY

It will be inferred from the preceding that unless we carefully define catholicity, we cannot call it a mark of The True Church. Such catholicity as Cardinal Gibbons, for example, claims for the Roman church is no mark of The Church. This church has sought to make itself *the only Church*, and thereby to earn the name " catholic."

How can mere extension constitute catholicity, as Gibbons urges? If this constitute catholicity then the apostolic church was not catholic.

As the word liberty may be claimed by a party who may be themselves far from free and who may enslave others, so the name " catholic " may be appropriated by a division of The Church which succeeds, in securing the mightiest organization and crushes out all weaker associations of Christians, till it seems almost alone. No one church has ever become catholic, in the one legitimate use of the word, as The Church which embraced all genuine Christians and all true churches. Even at the time of its earliest success there were those called autokephaloi, who refused to accept the domination of the then triumphing " Catholic " organization. The definition of catholic in the Roman Catechism is almost absurd : " The Church is styled catholic because all who wish to attain salvation must hold and embrace her."

The word catholic is not used in connection with The Church until the middle of the second century (Ign. ad Smyrn., 8). The meaning has since been much disputed. Some say it means the inner oneness of The Church which makes it to be unaffected by outer divisions ; The Church is catholic because it everywhere manifests all its attributes. This in Möhler's idea (see Köstlin in Herzog I, V, p. 699), and Vincent of Lorens has given the famous dictum for the Church : *quod semper, quod ubique, quod ab omnibus.*

Correctly, catholic means the whole, or the universal Church, as over against a particular church ; as the bishop is head of a single church so is Christ head of the universal Church. (See Ignatius.)

It was only in later usage that the word " catholic " designated the church which the Roman government recognized as over against separated or heretical churches. This named the attempt to identify, by means of this word, a part of The Church with the whole, and to exclude from the Church such Christians and churches as had no place within The Church recognized by the Roman government. Thus, the word " catholic" was perverted and ceased to mean catholic in its true and original sense. To bring all Christians into one organization has been a dream haunting many great minds. This partial catholicity was a terrible temptation, and became the source of innumerable ills. Catholicity was a condition which, carried of necessity its own dangers and soon led to the evils to which power in human hands almost invariably leads. No church is catholic in the sense of being the whole Church, or of including all Christians. " Catholicity" became sectarian in limiting itself within bounds narrower than those Christ appointed. However much it might pour contempt on some small group of independent Christians, even in its derision it was uncatholic. No church, indeed no number of organized churches, can have true catholicity because the moment organization takes place exclusion begins, and the established church becomes one of many churches. As if a power should take of the ocean and put a barrier across some great bay or gulf, it would thereby separate this gulf from the

ocean and so far cease to be the ocean—so every
church by its barriers of creed and custom separates
itself so far forth from The Truly Catholic Church.
The Donatists said correctly: " Catholic " is a *geographical* designation.

*The only Catholic Church is the whole body of Christ,
and the body of Christ includes all joined to Christ by
faith.* Only of this totality can catholicity be predicated, of the " general assembly and church of the first-
born." If the Roman church includes all living Christians, or if the Greek, or if the Reformed churches,
then whatever church does, this is catholic. But such
assertion would not now be made seriously by any
sane person. *A church which excludes by its own decisions a single person who is a member of Christ ceases
to be catholic.* The only Catholic Church is therefore
that body seen by Jesus Christ in its entirety and making
itself visible to man in the churches, so far as these are
composed of God's true children.

3. SANCTITY

Sanctity is an easily misunderstood and misapplied
mark of The Church. For example, when Cardinal
Gibbons claims that the Roman Catholic church is
especially holy, and when he says " the private lives
of Luther, and Calvin, and Knox, were stained by
cruelty, rapine and licentiousness," he must have been
thinking of some of the popes who were monsters of
iniquity and called children of hell by Roman Catholics
themselves. Such a statement as this of Cardinal
Gibbons is dangerous, both because it is false and

because it calls attention to a feature of Roman
Catholicism which we are all glad to forget, if we are
permitted.

But "sanctity" as a mark of The Church does not
mean sanctification, but means that Christians are
"called to be saints." If the lack of holiness in individual lives destroyed the reality of The Church, there
is and there can be no Church. True, all who are
called to be saints are becoming saints. Yet many
fail to attain. The Church is holy only because it is
set apart to holiness, and this mark is not easily discerned. Though, sooner or later the Spirit of God
within appears without. It certainly requires great
audacity in either a Roman or a Greek Catholic to
claim any other holiness, for neither of these churches
have distinguished themselves for purity and holiness
and sanctity.

It cannot be said that even the worship of these
churches is pure. The worship of the catholic
churches is largely corrupted and widely removed from
that simplicity which early marked Christian worship.

Harnack has written of the Greek (Orthodox)
church ("Das Wesen," pp. 137–8): "This church appears not as a Christian creation with a Grecian
veneer, but a Grecian creation with a Christian veneer.
If we strike out of its worship a few words, like Christ,
nothing reminds us further of a Christian origin"
(p. 137). Even the friendly Dean Stanley says of its
worship: "The mystical gestures, the awe which
surrounds the sacerdotal function, its long repetitions,
the severance of the sound from the sense, of the mind

from the act, both in priest and people, are not less, but more, remarkable than in the churches in the West." " Pictures are still retained and adored with even more veneration than the corresponding objects of devotion in the West, although statues are rigidly excluded. The same Greek monk who will ridicule the figures and even the bas-reliefs of a Roman Catholic Church will fling his incense and perform his genuflections with the most undoubting faith before the same saint as seen in the painting of his own convent cell " (Stanley, " Oriental Church ").

The Church, and all churches, contain those whose character abides far short, it may be, of perfection and sanctity of this sort.

There may be, in every separate church, many who are not called of God ; many who are not saints. No single church dare call itself holy. No one church is holy. The churches to whom the spirit spake in Revelation were unholy, yet had not yet ceased to contain true saints. The catholic churches, as well as the evangelic, have never lacked a multitude of true saints. But all churches are corrupted. " There is none holy, no not one."

As to the claims of superior sanctity of the catholic churches, the evangelical can let history speak. As we have already said, it is in America, not in Italy ; in England, not in Spain ; in Germany, not in Austria, that catholicism is purest, most free from faults which have too largely corrupted the catholic religion. The Roman Catholic church bears too strongly the image of Cæsar to bear in full beauty the image of Christ.

4. APOSTOLICITY

Apostolicity is not a matter of so-called apostolic succession in priesthood or ministry. The word "apostolic," in its earliest use, described such churches as either owed their existence to apostolic ministry or which sprang again from such churches. Tertullian says (Prescrip. Ag. Heresies XX), " They then in like manner founded churches in every city from which all the other churches, one after another, derived the tradition of the faith and the seeds of doctrine and are every day deriving them that they may become churches. Indeed, it is on this account only that they will be able to deem themselves apostolic as being the offspring of apostolic churches. Every sort of thing must revert to its original for its classification. Therefore the churches, although they are so great and so many, comprise but the one primitive church founded by the apostles, from which they all spring." These are remarkable words.

This, then, is the first essential, according to Tertullian, that a church be apostolic: it must owe its origin to the apostles, or to churches which the apostles founded. On this principle no Christian church can be deprived of this name, since it owes its birth indirectly, as the church at Antioch, at Rome, in Britain, to some original preaching of the Gospel by some missionary disciple of Christ, beginning from the Day of Pentecost.

When Tertullian adds (XXI) that only what the apostles preached is true doctrine and that *this is to be found in churches which they personally established,* he errs, since even the church in Jerusalem was never a pure fountain of doctrine and soon became Ebionitic. What the churches in Asia became, despite Paul and John, the Book of Revelation tells us. Apostolic foundation does not exclude Satanic doctrine (Rev. 3 : 9). Tertullian himself departed from the doctrine taught by the church called " apostolic." But, probably, Tertullian would have us understand that apostolicity is the characteristic of a church only so far as it truly, faithfully maintains the *original* doctrine in an apostolic church. He says, " all doctrine must be judged false which is contrary to the truth of the churches " (he does not say *the* Church), " and the apostles of Christ and God."

Many have laid emphasis on the supposed fact that the bishops were treasurers of the truth. Irenæus says that bishops have preserved the truth. He refers to that " tradition which originates from the apostles and which is preserved by means of the succession of presbyters in the churches " (Ag. Heresies, III, 2, 2).

In this respect he clearly gives precedence to the church at Rome which, he says (an opinion not upheld by the facts), Peter and Paul *founded.* We may admit that the churches which the apostles established *should* have continued in purity of doctrine. As a matter of fact, we know *they did not.* Nothing is more easily corrupted than tradition. Irenæus says: " It is not necessary to seek the truth among others which it is easy to obtain from the church, since the apostles like a rich man, in a bank, lodged in her hands most copiously all things pertaining to the truth " (*Ibid.*, IV, 1). But he adds: "*If the apostles themselves had not left us writings, would it not be necessary* to follow the course of tradition which they handed down to these to whom they did commit the churches?" Here writings are put above the tradition of presbyters. We have apostolic writings immeasurably preferable to tradition. The purpose and thought of both Irenæus and Tertullian is correct: We must, to be apostolic, be true to apostolic teaching. But, this teaching has not been kept pure in tradition. Tradition is not a trustworthy source of truth.

The writings of the apostles, or of the apostolic age, alone enable us to ascertain what apostolic truth is, and this truth *as recorded* must be the test of the apostolicity of any church, and not what has descended by hearsay and vocal report.

We have then the only two tests of apostolicity, a church must be born by means of the Word, and a church must be true to apostolic teaching.

No one church can claim exclusive birthright, since all churches, if they be not merely nominally such, are made up of *individuals* who are begotten of the Word of truth. *It must be remembered that the Word does not create churches but Christians.* It generates life in individuals and these form churches. In this, therefore, it is clear that the truly apostolic, or better, the truly Christian Church (for the apostles were fallible men, Peter not excepted), is the One Church of all the "first-born" found in all the churches. And also this Church is the only truly Christian church, since being made up of God-begotten souls, it maintains actually that faith and hope and love which, often and unhappily, are hidden from sight beneath traditions and concealed in creeds and forms of man's invention.

While, as we have seen, the marks of unity, sanctity, catholicity and apostolicity (we need waste no time over infallibility which Gibbons has the effrontery to add) do not outwardly characterize any church, nor make evident The True Church, yet there is, as partly suggested, an apostolicity, sanctity and unity about The Church which is genuinely catholic.

The apostolicity is that already indicated by Tertullian: the fact that The Church owes its existence and abides faithful to the doctrine of the apostles as these represented Jesus Christ. The sanctity or holiness of The Church consists in the fact that it is composed of Christians who are called of God to sanctification through the Spirit.

5. THE TRUE UNITY OF THE CHURCH

Concerning the unity or oneness of The True Church, a few words further should be written.

There is an evangelic unity far more real than the catholic.

The error of the catholic is in supposing that the unity of The Church is necessarily an organic or secular unity of all Christians in some particular church. The essential unity of The Church was a fact which Paul realized, because The Church was the body of Christ. Nevertheless this unity of The Church did not bring with it in his day the unity of the churches.

Nor has it come in our day.   Paul never strove after organic or governmental union of the churches.   He gives no hint that the unity of The Church depended on the uniformity of all churches.   The church at Antioch was not in organic relation with the church at Rome.   When Victor of Rome asserted authority over other churches it was resented as an intrusion which other churches could not admit.

It is an odd admission when Moberly says: " The unity of the church was from the first a necessary *theological* principle and *was put into practice to the utmost extent that circumstances would allow* " (P. 18). Yet this is true.   Uniformity was a matter of circumstances.   Circumstances might not allow secular unity. To any open eye it is the plainest of all facts that circumstances have never allowed church unity in the sense of all Christians being in one visible Episcopal society.   There was complete independence of all the primitive churches.

Cardinal Gibbons defines the unity of The Church as " unity in the same doctrines of revelation and in the acknowledgment of the authority of the same pastor."

But this notion of unity, which is also that held by the catholic party in the Anglican church is not that which Paul held nor had it any expression in any writing of the first hundred years after Christ.

Hort, as against Moberly and Gore, and with Lightfoot and Hatch, is correct in saying that Paul does not establish nor notice any formal connection between different churches.   " Each is a body of Christ and a sanctuary of God."   It is true Paul anxiously promoted friendly intercourse and sympathy between scattered ecclesiæ, but this is not secular oneness, it is spiritual, though none the less a fact for that.

The error of the high churchmen is that they seem not to understand that a *spiritual union* of Christians and churches, *in one faith, hope and love*, can be both a fact, and a visible fact, amid superficial differences of organization.

Hatch says, correctly, " We see those to whom the Word of life was preached, gradually coalescing into societies." Moberly says, we must choose between a " unity by degrees from below" or "inherently from above." He uses "from below" and "from above" in an altogether misleading sense. Gradual unity through the operation of the Spirit is from above, while unity enforced by an organization is from below. The unity of the churches has never been an outwardly fixed affair. There is unity constantly contending with a spirit of disunion.

The unity of The Church was from above, from God. It was also from within, it is the unity of faith, hope and love, and not of bands of government. Tertullian in his day saw this. The Church is one because " of the same teaching of the same faith." " All is that one first church while the fellowship of peace and the title of brotherhood and the interchange of hospitality remain among them." Paul teaches, " the common bond of all Christians is Christ in them, the fellowship of Him" (I Cor. I: 2). So Hodge correctly says, " The Church is one because it embraces all the people of God" (o. c., 25).

When we look at The Church, in the first century, we see that its unity was more beneath the surface than visible. There were sharp contentions while Christ was on the earth in the flesh, and after He was present by the Spirit. The disciples agreed not in their desires. They differed in their doctrines. Peter and Paul represented what became distinct factions of The Church.

The Church at Corinth was a sample of The Church as a whole.

The prayer of Jesus was " that they *may* be one." He does not assert that they are one.

Yet the Christians were one as over against the non-Christian world. The discords and differences separated them in some degree from one another, yet as in any family, the blood of Christ, the spirit of Christ, gave them visible unity before the world. More and more the Christians were classed together, recognized as one and persecuted as one.

The unity of the early Church was the natural or spiritual oneness of soul, mind, heart. (On this see Hort, p. 120 ff., and McGiffert, pp. 636, 640 ff.)

The same rules for the union of Christians in *a* church as at Corinth (see 1 Cor. 4 : 14–17; 7 : 17; 11 : 16; 16 : 1; 14 : 33; 14 : 36) tended to keep the outward unity of Christians in the whole Church. The union was " the fellowship of Him " (1 Cor. 1 : 2).

As Köstlin says (Herzog, p. 695) " the union of the separate congregations in one church came not to appearance in any one form of church government. The unity appeared in universal and free fellowship

of Christian brotherly love. To this contributed especially the alms which Paul collected for the Jerusalem church, the apostolic exhortation to hospitality
and the greetings which Paul sent from one church to
another." (See 1 Cor. 1 : 11; 16: 17; Rom. 16: 17;
Titus 3: 10; Heb. 13 : 23; 3 John 6.)

How far removed is such spiritual oneness from that
secured in the " catholic " churches, by the crushing
and damning process !

The union was ethical. Immorality was a justifi-
able ground for breaking the fellowship, and the denial
of Jesus as the Christ was ground for separation, yet
in a spirit of *brotherly love*. (See 1 Cor. 5 : 9; 2 Thess.
3: 14, 15; Phil. 1 : 5 ; 2: 1; Gal. 6: 1; Acts 2: 42.)

Thus there was real unity—never outwardly perfect
—long before any Roman Catholic church or Episcopal
society arose. There was no oneness of outward conformity certainly for two centuries, in fact has never
been. The only unity which in the New Testament
is regarded as worth striving after, is the oneness
which comes to outwardness because it is an inward
fact. Anything like outward constraint in securing
religious unity is false to New Testament teachings.
Any other constraint than that of love the apostles
following Christ disdain to use. The expulsion of a
sinful brother, or rather the withdrawal from such,
does not justify compulsion nor persecution. It
should not, must not, be done except in love. No
violence must be used. Paul's zeal for the purity of
the Church at Corinth was that of one who loved even
him who had offended. (See 2 Cor. 7: 9.) Hence the

methods of the "catholic" church, and sometimes of the protestant churches as well, to secure unity are condemned. A unity which is maintained by *any* force whether physical or mental or so-called moral, is not unity, but uniformity. All genuine Christians and therefore all true churches are one in certain respects, freely and voluntarily. As is said in Ephesians (4 : 2) there is a unity which every Christian will keep, it is the unity which comes from the Father, the Son and the Spirit. There is one body, one spirit, one hope. There is one Lord, one faith, one baptism. There is one God and Father, in all, through all, over all.

This and this only is Church or Christian unity. Whoever breaks this unity ceases to be a member of the one Church, which cannot be divided in its essence. There can be but one Church, since there is only one Spirit, only one Christ, only one Father.

This unity is visible, if not always when we look upon the surface of the Church yet always when we look on its boundary. The Church, all Christians, all except nominal Christians, are one, over against the non-Christian world,—not against the non-Christian world in hate, but in love. As true Israel of old was separate from the Philistines, from Moabites, from Syrians, so the true Israel of to-day is separate from the heathen world which lieth in wickedness. So far, it is one and visible.

The States of our Union are all one as over against any foreign nation. They may be divided among themselves.

A family is one, even though brother is alienated for a time from brother.

Christians as a fact are one because " all ye are brethren " ; all have one Father; there is only one household of faith ; only one temple of the Holy Ghost.

But when we look upon the churches, upon Christians as members of churches in relation one to another, there is not perfect unity. There was not among the disciples when Christ was on earth. There was not among the apostles after His departure. There has never been. It is a prayer yet to be answered; that all may be one, in the full fellowship of love.

It is the seeking of the other mode of unity, the outward and compulsory which has brought divisions into The Church.

For the unity of all Christians in life and action as well as in creed and cultus Christ served and prayed when on earth. For this and no other unity Paul and every other Christ-filled disciple strives and prays. Paul's endeavours are traced in vivid lines on the history of his labours. He strove to bring all Christians together.

Such oneness is impossible if faith be a subtle mixture of human philosophy and divine revelation. All Christians can have one faith, one belief; that is, one attitude of heart and mind towards Jesus Christ only as this attitude is simple, unmixed, pure. Whoever adds an unessential doctrine which is perplexing, confusing, doubt-creating, offends against the unity of The Church, divides superficially at least, the body of Christians.

Unity shall ultimately prevail when men cease to be as " children tossed to and fro and carried about with every wind of doctrine, by the sleight of men and cunning craftiness " (Eph. 4 : 14).

The second element of this unity is the " one hope of your calling." All Christians and therefore all churches and the whole Church is and are one in hope. This hope is the coming of the Kingdom of God and of His Christ.

The Church has remained truer and therefore more visibly one in hope than in faith.   There have indeed been differences far reaching in effect.   The development of individualistic conceptions of salvation soon debased the catholic church.   Then came purely selfish notions of salvation, when each individual sought to save himself as from a doomed and cursed world regardless of the fate of his fellow men.   The " catholic" church became a vast ark in which men felt themselves safe from the floods of divine wrath.   The purpose of The Church, to carry the Gospel to all nations, changed to the purpose of making a church, a vast organization in which alone, rather than through the saving power of the truth, man was to be saved.   Believing itself to be the Kingdom of God rather than *the voice* to call them to Christ and the Kingdom, The Church laboured for its own growth and aggrandizement, its own power and glory.   Others, and sometimes the same persons, forgetting that the Kingdom is yet to come, have satisfied themselves with the notion that in the steady improvement of man's earthly condition was the realization of this Kingdom.   While still others have gone to an opposite extreme and have ceased to work that the earth might be ready for the final revelations of the King and His Kingdom in their eagerness to escape from earth unto the glory of heaven, preferring to go to the Kingdom rather than to wait and work for it on earth. Yet the true hope has never ceased to underlie and pervade even false forms of it and the whole Church, as Paul said to the Thessalonians, is waiting "for His Son from heaven, whom He raised from the dead, even Jesus which delivered us from the wrath to come." And every true Christian worker, as he may be able to bring others from darkness to light, says with Paul, "for what is our hope or joy, or crown of rejoicing. Are not even ye in the presence of our Lord Jesus Christ at His coming?" (1 Thess. 2 : 19).

The third and last element of unity in the True Church is love. "Now abideth faith, hope, charity, the greatest of these is charity." God is love, whoever is begotten of God loves. Every Christian is growing in love. The whole Church is bound together by love, love to God which must if it exist, so far as it exists, manifest itself in love to man. The Apostle Paul was most eager to secure true Church oneness in true fellowship. When Paul left James and Peter and John at Jerusalem these latter gave to him and Barnabas the right hand of fellowship, and recommended to them the poor of the Jerusalem church. These were the two chief manifestations of love; fellowship and charity.

The exercise of hospitality was a bond which long held Christians together in a unity which unhappily was later somewhat broken, through the hardening of The Church into a rigidity of rules and dogmas. The Church was knit together as the meshes of a net by the welcome a Christian found wherever there was a brother Christian (Rom. 12:13; 1 Pet. 4:9; Heb. 13:2; 3 John 5–8).

Paul was himself the greatest bearer of salutations (1 Cor. 16:19; Rom. 16:4, 6; Phil. 4:22). His endeavour was not to connect all the churches as links in a chain are connected so much as to fuse them together in the flame of the divine fire of love. He pours it out as liquid fire in the great chapter on charity, which is the perfect bond. So John taught that love was brotherliness.

The prayer of all Christians is expressed in the beautiful prayer given in the Didache for use at the communion service:

"Even as the broken bread was scattered over the hills and was gathered together and become one, so let Thy Church be gathered together from the ends of the earth into Thy Kingdom."

We conclude: Christ Jesus in a church, is the one and only mark of The Church. Louis XIV said: "I am the state." Jesus alone can say: "I am The Church." "Where two or three are gathered in My name, there am I." Where Christ is, there is The Church. Where Jesus is, there will be unity, sanctity, catholicity.

The unity will be a unity which requires no outward band to make it real; it will be a unity of which Christ alone is cause and attracting centre.

The sanctity will not be an outward sanctity, the obedience of any external commandments, but the outflow into life of the spirit that is in the heart.

The catholicity will be that universality wherewith Christ belongs to all and all belongs to Him.

The apostolicity will be the permanent abiding of Christians in the doctrine and life delivered by Christ, through His spirit, to the disciples, called also apostles, and transmitted through prophets and teachers working by the Holy Spirit.

THE MISSION OF THE CHURCH

———

Jesus Christ exemplifies this.

1. *The Kingly Mission of Jesus and The Church.*
    To subdue man to God.
    The Kingdom as future.
    The Kingdom as "coming" and as "come."
    Its blessedness experienced now.
    The Kingdom is brought to man.
    Man is brought to the Kingdom.
    The Church must conquer the world.

2. *The priestly work of Jesus and The Church.*
    The growth of a sacerdotal society.
    The Church has no "sacerdotal" duty.
    The Church offers spiritual sacrifices.
    Jesus Christ offers Himself.
    The true nature of Christian sacrifices.
    New Testament silence as to priestly functions.
    This Moberly admits.
    The true worship of God by the eucharist.
    Worship is the whole of sacrifice.
    The symbolic use of the eucharist.
    The danger of priestcraft.
    The Anglican priest has "nothing to offer."

3. *The Prophetic Work of The Church.*
    The prophet the representative servant of God.
    The place of the prophet in The Church.
    The threefold work of The Church.

XV

THE MISSION OF THE CHURCH

THE true concept of The Church is to be discovered in the work assigned to it by its Head, Christ Jesus.

Whatever is necessary to the fulfillment of its mission is essential to The Church.

Whatever is not necessary to its functional activity is not necessary to the being of The Church. Therefore we inquire: What is the mission of The Church? The original and perpetual office or mission of The Church is found in the life work of Jesus Christ. This has its earliest illustration in the activity of the apostles and the churches which they established. All the activity of Christ was the outflow of His faith, His hope, His love. All the activity of The Church has these as its permanent source.

It is clear that Jesus Christ expected His disciples to do His work as preparatory to the sharing of His glory, just as He did His Father's work.

1. THE KINGLY WORK OF CHRIST AND THE CHURCH

Jesus Christ came to be the King of men ruling in a spiritual domain. "My kingdom is not of this world." It is not a kingdom made visible by rulers or governors nor maintained by any force, in outward

show of power. It is a kingdom of the Spirit, of
truth, of righteousness. Christ said, the Kingdom does
not come with observation. He did not mean that it
did not make itself felt or seen. He meant that it
came from within, from above, and, ultimately, would
be a surprise in its full glory.

The Kingdom of God is to come. It is coming.
The Church, like Christ on earth, is at work hastening
that advent.

The office of a king pertained to the Lord Jesus
not in the sense of one who had come into His Kingdom, but of one who is winning His Kingdom. It
was certainly not a dominion which had its expression
in any pomp or power of a material sort. It was a
kingship of character, a dominion of the spirit. As
such He lives and reigns. Like Him, all His followers
are to be kings. They are to rule in a spiritual her-
itage. The kingly mission of The Church is to subdue all things to God. This was and is the work of
the spirit of Christ. " Then cometh the end when He
shall have delivered up the kingdom to God, when He
shall have annihilated all (alien) rule and authority and
power."

The Church inherits this work of Jesus Christ. It
has a kingly function. The kingdoms of this world
are to become the Kingdom of God and of His
Christ.

The purpose of Jesus as Lord of the Church, as
King in God's Kingdom, was dual. It was *the bringing of a people into that Kingdom and the bringing
of the Kingdom to this redeemed people.*

The coming of the Kingdom, as Jesus taught it, is
distinctly an affair of the future, as Köstlin says.   This
is more and more recognized by students of primitive
Christianity. (See McGiffert, p. 41 ff.)

Meyer says that Jesus always speaks of the Kingdom as in the future and its coming as apocalyptic.
This is true so far as the actual advent of the Kingdom of glory is concerned.   Jesus did not come to
establish a new kingdom.   There is not a word in the
New Testament justifying the supposition that He
did.   As to its subjects, this Kingdom is of old.   It
can hardly be deduced from the words: " My kingdom is not of this world," nor in the acceptance of the
title of King; nor is it shown by the words: " the
Kingdom of God is among you."   This is the correct
translation, and not " within you," which is mystical
language such as Jesus never used.   The probable
meaning of this sentence, as the context shows, is, the
Kingdom will come so suddenly, at the last, like the
lightning, that one will not be able to say, Lo here! or,
Lo there! for behold, instantly, the Kingdom of God is
among you.   Jesus is speaking of the final advent.

The Kingdom of God may, indeed must, be thought
of in two ways (1) as a coming reality in glory-
form when God shall come in Christ, in Messianic
glory ; and (2) as perpetually coming in all the operations of God's grace and goodness among men.   In
this latter sense the Kingdom did not begin to come
with Christ, it began when " the first man stood, God
conquered, with face to Heaven upturned."   It began
immediately when man was born as child of God, and

in varying measure has been coming ever since in
every blessing God has sent to men as object of His
favouring grace. Jesus Christ is necessarily the one
through whom, to man, the blessedness of the Kingdom is most given in all its progressive stages. In this
sense He is the Messiah. So that while the Kingdom
is future to John and future to Jesus even in the night
before His death, when He says He will no more
drink of the fruit of the vine until He drink it in the
Kingdom of God, yet it is also true that some of the
power and some of the blessedness of the Kingdom is
present even when Jesus is in His state of humility.
As He says: " If I by the finger of God cast out devils
then is the Kingdom of God come unto you." Which
indeed means no more than if one looking at the glow-
ing east and the light spreading over the earth and the
shadows fleeing away, should say that the sun is on
earth even before it is risen in its full orbed splendour.

Thus the Kingdom was felt even though not fully
come. Jesus came to bring it *all*, but man was un-
ready for it. Its complete advent was impossible, but
Jesus Christ, and any child of God, cannot be on
earth without bringing, in some measure, the blessings of the Kingdom, especially in the casting out of
all which may be called devilish. " Ye are the salt
of the earth, the light of the world." This work Jesus
committed to His disciples. For this, the instruction
to the Twelve and to the Seventy is clear evidence.
The disciples are to heal and help, as well as to preach
the Gospel. Everything, in fact, which can minister
to man's well-being is duty to the Christian and there-

fore to The Church. As Christ came to minister and
to give His life a ransom, so must each in his own degree do likewise (Matt. 20 : 28).

The second part of the work of Christ, as King, and
therefore of The Church, is the bringing of others into
the Kingdom, that is, making them its subjects by the
proclamation of the good news, calling them to faith,
to hope, to love.

Preparatory to this faith and hope and love is re-
pentance or the abandonment of the old life of unbelief and despair and selfishness. To proclaim this
gospel was the work of Christ and it is the work of
His Church. As preparation for the Kingdom, the
nurture of Christians in Church fellowship is required.
To this end, are the means of grace which God, in
Christ, by His Spirit, has committed to The Church
for its growth into the full stature of Jesus Christ.

The Church must rule the world, must conquer it,
subdue it to and for God. It must cast down all that
opposes itself to God ; till, in Christ's name and power,
every knee is willingly bent in His honour, till all
things are put under Him and God is all and
in all.

This office The Church fulfills not by carnal means,
never by force, but in the meekness which shall inherit
the earth. As Paul says (2 Cor. 10 : 4), " We do not
war after the flesh. For the weapons of our warfare
are not carnal." Again, " Approving ourselves as the
ministers of God in much patience, in afflictions, in
necessities, in distresses, in stripes, in imprisonments,
. . . by pureness, by knowledge, by long suffering,

by kindness, by the Holy Spirit, by love unfeigned "
(2 Cor. 6 : 4–7).

So far as the Kingdom of God is concerned, whatever advantages do undoubtedly result from the organization of Christians into an army-like oneness, yet
this unity of an outward sort under a one visible com-
mander has never been true of The Church and is not
essential to the existence of The Church.   It may well
be that The Church can conquer the world more
effectively by its different organizations, than by any
premature and immature oneness.   The diversities of
gifts, and diversities of operations (1 Cor. 12) will, almost of necessity, find expression in many varying
forms of Church life and service, each contributing to
the conquest of the world.

2.   THE PRIESTLY WORK OF THE CHURCH

The Kingdom of God indicates, as no other one phrase
does, what is the work of The Church, as Christ committed it to His disciples.   They were to go into all
the world and preach the Gospel of the Kingdom,
teaching all nations to observe His commandments,
with the assurance of His abiding presence until the
end of the age should come and He return in Messianic
glory to receive the kingdoms of this world as His
own, and all should be in subjection to God the Father.

But, this simple work which Peter and the other
disciples carried forward after Christ's departure, to
which Paul consecrated his great ability, has during
the subsequent centuries been greatly neglected for a
false priestly work, and contrary to Christ's original

teaching. The Church became, during the thousand years between the fifth and fifteenth centuries, a mighty sacerdotal society. Sacerdotalism is almost a synonym for catholicism.

To understand the true sacerdotalism of The Church is not difficult, if one is willing to learn or see, and refuses to be confused by the clamours and contentions of priests.

The priest has ever been the often unconscious and unwitting enemy of pure religion. Priestcraft has its source and power in the not unnatural fear that man has of God. " When I consider, I am afraid of Him," says Job, and fear before God is a sacred and worthy emotion. But, priestcraft is not the way to profit by that fear.

The New Testament is absolutely silent as to the sacerdotal function of The Church, *in the sense of the priestly activity* of the Jewish and the catholic churches.

In this sense, of performing services which tend to propitiate God, to offer sacrifices which seek to bring man into favour with God, there is no priestly activity discernible in the Apostolic Church. This is too well known to need extended proof. Indeed, the word priest is not used at all with reference to the Christian. In I Peter we read that The Church is a holy, a royal priesthood (like David or Solomon), but it is immediately stated, so as to render all uncertainty inexcusable, " *to offer up spiritual sacrifices.*" Sacrifice, in the New Testament sense, is a clear idea. It is the service man renders to God by means of the body (Rom. 12 : 1); Paul pours forth his life upon the sacrifice and

service which the Philippian Christians performed
(Phil. 2 : 17); the fruit of our lips, the sacrifice of
praise, is offered unto God (Heb. 13 : 15). When the
saints are called priests in the book of Revelation, it is
as kings who can stand before God and all worship
Him. There is no thought of sacrifice. It is only as
offerers of worship and service of a spiritual kind that
the Christian is a priest. In this sense all Christians
form a "royal priesthood." He has no sacrifice, in the
common sense of that word, to offer. Almsgiving
is an acceptable sacrifice to God (Phil. 4 : 18); but all
that God receives is the spirit and not the thing; that
is offered to man. It is not a sacrifice as was understood in the Old Testament. The *thing* is given to
man; the *spirit* is what God sees and receives.

Therefore the notion that The Church has any
priestly function other than that of pure worship of
God in spirit and in truth is utterly without warrant,
indeed contradictory to the teaching of Jesus and the
disciples.

It is therefore dangerous when Lindsay calls The
Church a sacerdotal society even though he qualifies
the word, limiting the sacrifices to spiritual offerings.

In whatever sense the priestly work of Jesus Christ
be regarded, it does away with all notion that the
Christian, whether called laicus or clerus, has any
priestly work other than the offering of spiritual worship.

The arguments upon which Canons Gore and Moberly, as well as catholics generally, lay so much stress,
that because Jesus was a priest therefore His minister

is a priest, instead of being valid or merely invalid, prove exactly the opposite. *Because Jesus was a priest and offered a perfect sacrifice there can be no more sacrifice and no further priesthood.* Only so far as the sacrifice of Jesus was an act of perfect worship; only so far as it was perfect holiness and creative of holiness is it susceptible of perpetual repetition. So far as it is regarded as expiatory it cannot be repeated nor continued. In this respect there can be but the one sacrifice. It is unique. Paul asks with warmth, even indignation, " Was Paul crucified for you ? " The Church is not as a whole, nor is any individual in it, a priest to offer up any sacrifice which can reconcile man to God. Man is reconciled to God, so far as that can be conceivably secured by any sacrifice. All further sacrifices have man, not God, as their object; as Paul says, they are " for Christ's body, The Church." God calls for the offering or sacrificing of the individual life and heart. But this has no effect other than that of example or ministry in securing the salvation of any other.

" There remains no more sacrifice for sin." To offer again that sacrifice, except as a symbol of what man would render to God, is a disparagement of its efficacy, is a denial of God's gracious mercy freely offered.

The New Testament contradicts in a hundred places, and never once teaches in even the shadowiest way, that The Church or any member in it, can or should think to offer that sacrifice again in any form, as an actual offering.

Therefore the calling of The Church a sacerdotal society is misleading, and, as commonly understood, is false.

The only acceptable "sacrifices" in the New Testament—and indeed in the genuinely Old Testament sense—are "spiritual sacrifices" (1 Pet. 2 : 5), "living sacrifices."

The Christian is to present his body (Rom. 12 : 1), the praise of his lips (Heb. 13 : 15), his possessions (Acts 24 : 17; Phil. 4 : 18).

The whole doctrine of the Christian sacrifice is beautifully taught in a somewhat difficult sentence of Paul's (Rom. 15 : 16) "that I should be the minister of Jesus Christ, to the Gentiles, ministering the Gospel of God that the offering up of the Gentiles might be acceptable, being sanctified by the Holy Ghost." Here Paul teaches that the Gentiles, through the sanctifying effect of the Gospel preached by him are his (Paul's) sacrifice to God. He offers, presents to God, as his sacrifice the multitude of sanctified Gentiles. Can there be any other offering so pleasing to God? Thus he worships God.

In enumerating the gifts God gave to The Church there is absolute silence in all the Pauline Epistles as to any "priestly" function.

Any sacrifice to appease God, to turn aside His wrath, the offering of the body and death of Jesus Christ as in the mass is more than a perversion of the truth, it is a taking away of the true sense of the Gospel.

Moberly (p. 87) admits that the word "priest" was not in use until the middle of the second century, and

Gore also says (p. 196), " Irenæus and Clement do not speak of the Christian ministers as priests, while Tertullian and Cyprian do, so that it is only towards the end of the second century that sacerdotal terms begin to be applied to the clergy," and even then not in a strictly sacerdotal sense.   Can anything be more evident than this, that sacerdotalism is not apostolic, not Christian?

Lightfoot has shown there was no priesthood in the early Christian Church.   There was no other offering than that of gifts to the poor, presented at the table of the Lord.   Incense was offered in praise, to signify the going up of man's devotion to God.   In this sense the bread and wine as Christ's body and blood, perpetually represent the devotion of The Church to God and man. But they are not sacrificed in any sacerdotal sense.   It was, further, not the act of the " priest " but of the whole Church and every individual.   The administrator did not even " represent " the Church as Moberly so earnestly maintains.   He is simply a minister.

It is true that the Eucharist is called a thusia, a sacrifice, in the Didache (14) and Justin Martyr says (Dial, XLI) they " offer sacrifices to Him, *i. e.*, the bread of the Eucharist and also the cup of the Eucharist."   But, that this was a sacrifice in the Levitical sense his reference to Malachi (1 : 11), disproves : " in every place *incense* shall be offered unto My name." The sacrifice is memorial and symbolic.

There is not a trace of sacerdotalism in the Ignatian letters.   The use of a word, sacrifice, in early Christian writings does not affirm that it was a fact that Christ was again sacrificed or even offered, in form, as a sacrifice. The act of partaking, of communing, was an act of worship and so was a sacrifice, for *as formerly sacrifice was the whole of worship, so in the New Testament worship is all of sacrifice.* Whoever worships God, offers Him praise, thereby sacrifices to Him.

In the Eucharist, the officiating minister may present the bread and the cup as the symbols of that perfect service which Jesus Christ rendered. Thus it may be a pure act of worship to present these symbols to God, as indicative of the purpose and intent of the worshipping Church.

But, there is so much danger in the use of the word, priest, as Lightfoot taught, that it were better to follow the New Testament, and not use it at all of our Church ministers. As Sanday says (p. 88) the development of priesthood " which began in the second century ended in the state of things before the Reformation." In Justin Martyr's account, the elements are handed around as in any modern protestant service.

Communion was certainly the first notion in connection with the Supper. It meant Christian fellowship. But, the idea of worship was never absent from it. The Church has priestly work in the worship of God, in presenting itself as a sanctified body to God. The sacrifice of Christ, as the perfect and ideal worship of God, becomes the symbol of all true worship. Only in a symbolic sense can the " supper " be an act of sacrifice and worship.

When Moberly affirms that because Christ was a priest therefore The Church is, he is misled by words.

Christ was not a priest in any other sense than in *offering Himself*, and so the Christian and The Church are " priests " only as offering the self to God. The fact is, in the Anglican church, the priest has nothing to offer in the catholic sense. In the Roman Catholic church the idea is consistently carried out and the Roman Catholic church properly enough despises the " Anglican priesthood " as being a priesthood without anything to sacrifice. And, we repeat, *the very fact that Christ was priest in the sense of offering a perfect sacrifice does away (as the letter to the Hebrews teaches) with all subsequent sacrifice and therefore priesthood.* Moberly says : " The Church is priestly because from her proceeds the aroma of perpetual offerings towards God. The Church is priestly because her arms are spread out perpetually to succour and intercede for those who need the sacrifice of love." This is true enough but this is the protestant and not the catholic meaning. But, while it is fact that The True Church, the real body of Christ, does send forth a sweet aroma of praise to God and succours man, yet this is entirely independent of any sacerdotal class. As history distinctly affirms, introduce the priestly caste into your religion and there is danger of illusion and delusion.

When, in his conciliatory fashion, Dr. Sanday (pp. 91, 92) calls attention to the sacrifice a minister *is*, this has not the remotest connection with a priest sacrificing the eucharist or mass. The word priest is too dangerous. Its use will certainly lead to priest-craft. The apostles knew as much as Cyprian. The word has no place in The Church except as naming the fact that *every* Christian is a *worshipper* who can come freely to God, as in the Old Testament a priest could do. It is also of moment to notice that The Church of the Old Testament was a far larger thing than that which found expression or manifestation in Levitical and priestly activities. Indeed, the Christian Church is learning far too slowly, that the priest of the earlier history of The Church no more represented the Hebrew religion than does the catholic priest of to-day represent the Christian Church.

3. THE PROPHETIC WORK OF THE CHURCH

Peter says: " He commanded us to preach to the people " (Acts 10 : 42). The apostles realized this as the last command of Jesus. The work for the Kingdom was by means of preaching and teaching (Matt. 28 : 19). Harnack, as well as most all students of Church history now recognize that the prophet held the first place in the Christian Church. The true representative of the ancient Church, as of the later Christian form, was the prophet. If this be not so, let any one parallel the great line of prophets from Samuel to Malachi with priests of equal right to stand as God's representatives. The prophet occupied the first place in the Christian Church. Indeed he alone really, actually, represented the spiritual activity of The Church, both on its Godward and its manward side. The prophet was the man of prayer as well as the man who proclaimed God's truth. No one could be an apostle who was not also a prophet. Jesus Christ came in the succession of John the prophet.

The chief function of the Church is prophetic, proclamatory, ambassadorial.

Even the rite of baptism and the fellowship of the supper are prophetic. It was prophets and not priests who baptised. It was prophets and not priests who, occupying a parental place in a communion of believers, served the elements of the supper.

The purpose of these so-called sacraments is not so priestly, as prophetic. They are for edification, to build up The Church.

The place occupied by the prophet in the early Church can hardly be exaggerated! Paul was a prophet, glorying in the fact. Polycarp was a prophet. Ignatius was a prophet. Cyprian and other pastors in North Africa had the same gift. The prophet was the centre of The Church under both dispensations. The effect of the Holy Spirit was to make prophets. Paul urges all to cultivate this gift. The Didache tells us the place the prophet held: " My child, him that speaketh to thee the Word of God, thou shalt have him in remembrance day and night and honour him as the Lord " (Did. IV: 1). The prophet administered the Lord's supper.

There was a narrower and a larger use of the word, covering a narrower and a larger service. In the narrower sense it named what was akin to the speaking with tongues. In the broader sense, it referred to the proclamation of the teaching of doctrine according to the teaching of Christ and the early disciples. The first is a transient gift, the second remains the permanent duty of The Church to the world.

Gradually the prophets of the so-called spiritual order passed away and permanent teachers took their place. Apostles, prophets and teachers were alike all preachers. As Paul said to himself: " God sent me to preach." The preaching function of The Church; the proclamation of the Gospel, with the edification of believers, and the practice of worship, all came to manifestation in the preaching pastor or bishop of the early Church.

Under the leadership of the pastor, The Church came to realize a threefold mission: towards the world without, towards itself within, towards God above. The Church had and has the threefold work, which is in relation to the Kingdom of God: evangelization, edification, worship. It is the threefold work of faith, hope and love.

XVI

THE MINISTRY OF THE CHURCH

How shall the Church execute its mission.
The Church operative as a whole.
There is no necessity of a clerical class.
The rights of laymen.
Paul's teaching on ministry.
The Church not, lay *and* clerical.
Hatch on growth of the clerical class.
Liddon on the purpose of endowments.
The schism wrought by clericalism.
A church may ordain its ministers.
Organization was an independent matter.
The Twelve did not appoint James.
Eusebius quoted.
Every local church has a right to organize.
The local church has all the power of The Church.
In what sense the ministry is from above.
The Church as a whole cannot abdicate.
Nor can any part of it.
All gifts from the same source.
Stephanus put himself into the ministry.
Charity will hinder schism.
The organization of a local church.
Material interests first demand regulation.
The waning of prophecy.
The necessity of orderliness.
The well-being of a church.

XVI

THE MINISTRY OF THE CHURCH

THE work of The Church, its functional activity, is
of the whole as collected individuals and not of any
class. The True Church can, in any local church, altogether apart from any set ministry, or any in " holy
orders," perform all its functions. The believers, and
not a ministry set apart, constitute The Church. The
setting apart of a ministry is a matter, it may be, of
the well-being but not of the being of a church. But
it may, frequently has, contributed to the ruin of a
church.

The Church performs all these services through its
members, through all its members, without distinction
of lay or clerical. No reader of the New Testament
can doubt that *every member of Christ's household has
His ministry and has the threefold ministry*. He
must and will, as a member of Christ, contribute according to the gift of Christ, to the total work of The
Church in the service of God, its service of self, its
service of mankind.

The separation of *some* of a community of Christians, be it a few, or be it many, to perform regularly
and continuously certain duties is purely a matter of
convenience, of expediency, not necessity.

Calvin is inconsistent with himself when he says
there is no church " without a ministry," unless

" ministry " mean, what it rightly does mean, the
service which *every* Christian is bound to perform,
and some, simply by way of eminence, may have
duties of supervision and directions.

We have already seen that, as Hatch says (p. 216),
the framing of Church organization is left to human
hands. He has shown that a so-called layman had a
right to perform any ecclesiastical function necessary
to Church life and activity (p. 125).

Paul evidently teaches that every member of a
church has ministerial duty to perform, " according as
God hath dealt to every man the measure of faith, for
we have many members in one body and all members
have not the same office " (Rom. 12 : 3, 4). All have
not the *same* office ; yet all have *an* office, and Paul
is not saying that though some exercise, through
peculiar endowment, a special duty, no one else
possesses the right to do the same according to the
measure of his gift. That is, *if one excel* as a prophet,
that does not mean that he alone is to prophesy. He
tells the Corinthians generally to cultivate this gift.
The right to exhort (Rom. 12 : 8) is no more exclusively one person's right than the right to give, which
is associated with it. And so Paul puts together the
ruling with diligence and the showing mercy with
cheerfulness. In other words Paul's ideal Church, as
pictured in Rom. 12, has no superior order. The
nearest to superiority is the prophet, because he serves
most. So in 1 Cor. 12, Paul considers a church as an
assembly of Christians among whom he sees as yet
no ruling class. In his usual love of the Trinity he

regards these gifts as source, as service, as results ; as source from the Spirit, as service with reference to Christ, as result with reference to God. He says clearly *the manifestation of the spirit is given to every one.* Not all the same, nor in the same measure, one has more wisdom, another more knowledge, another more faith, another healing power, another miraculous power, another prophetic ability, another discernment of spirits, another ecstatic tongue power, another interpretation of tongues (1 Cor. 12 : 8–10).

Thus The Church is not divided into lay and clerical, ordained and unordained, but The Church has many varied activities all of which must be kept in order as he is at pains to tell them, since God is not the author of confusion.

It is evident that *Paul here knows no ministerial class.* The Church has no ministers *over* it, but servants *within* it.

The growth of the clerical class has been clearly and unmistakably sketched by Hatch. There were three main causes. The doctrine concerning infant baptism lowered the moral tone of the church membership, the notion of order was derived from the Roman state, the catholic sought to make the catholic church resemble the Jewish church.

The state came in with positive aid. It passed laws affecting the clergy, it made them independent by allowing the catholic church to hold property and by endowing churches. Monasticism introduced a peculiar notion of clerical morals and tended to the isolation of the clergy.

As Hatch (p. 124) says, "little by little those members of the Christian churches who did not hold office
were excluded from the performance of almost all ecclesiastical functions.   At first a layman might not
preach if a bishop were present; then not if any
church officer were present; and finally not at all.   At
first a layman brought his own gifts to the altar and
communicated there, and then he could only stand
outside the dais upon which the officers sat or stood;
and finally, in the Eastern church, he might not even
see the celebration of the Mysteries."

Yet, Tertullian says: "are not our laics priests?"
(Chastity c. vii).   And, whatever extravagances Tertullian may have fallen into, he had a correct conception of the ministry.

This class-clergy is distinctly post-apostolic, and so
far as it is made a necessity in any church it tends to
separate that church from the one true apostolic
Church.   There may be advantages for a church to
have a self-perpetuating ministerial class, yet the root,
however deep in antiquity, is the voluntary consent of
a community of Christians.   This may be obscured
and forgot, yet is a fact.

Diversities of gifts and operations do not justify class
distinction as lay and clergy.   This, Canon Liddon
admits, "the difference between clergy and laity is in
a difference of the degree in which certain spiritual
powers are conferred, not in a difference in kind"
(p. 90).   His attempt to break the force of this admission is not successful: "Spiritual endowments are
given to the Christian laymen with one purpose, to

the Christian ministry with another purpose. The object of the first is personal, that of the second is corporate." This latter statement is wrong. The only
purpose wherefore, according to Paul, God gives any
one a gift, it is for use not personal but for the whole
body. (See Eph. 4.) It is just here, by the "high"
church separation of The Church into two parts, lay
and clerical, that a virtual schism is wrought and the
purpose of the Holy Ghost is contradicted. This is
the most fatal of all schisms.

When the "high" churchman (and sometimes
the Presbyterian is "high" church in this respect)
denies that a gift from God is equivalent to its use,
then the whole purpose of the gift is nullified. But,
any church or community of Christians has a right
because of the power given to *it*, to determine *so far
as itself* is concerned, by any God-inspired method,
whether that gift is to be exercised upon or among
that church. Since self-deception as to the fact of a
divine gift is possible, a church, itself should judge this
and recognize any gift, and in some way recognize and
ordain that gift for its use in that church. Sometimes
a church may err, as the Anglican church did in the
case of the brothers John and Charles Wesley. But,
the recognition of God's gift to any one cannot be left
absolutely to any class of men as distinct from the
whole Church. Paul would probably never have been
received by the apostles as a brother Christian unless
his success had compelled it.

The so-called corporate church may choose to act
through representatives and allow these to choose its

superior servants, or at least judge as to the qualifications. But this should never be so as to lessen the actual right and power reposed by God in the body of individual believers. It should never be that the church cannot act except through those whose action is independent of the volition of a church as a whole.

For such reasons the distinction of two classes in a church, a hierarchy and the laity, has been and always will be vicious, both to those who are in the so-called higher class and those in the so-called lower class. It sets up two religions, two kinds of religious conduct.

History shows us clearly that, at first, the churches exercised *self*-government and only little by little did those who had been the servants of a church become its masters.

As Lindsay says (p. 132), the churches "starting from the simplest forms of combination they framed their ministry to serve their own needs in accordance with what they saw was best suited for their own peculiar work."

The church at Jerusalem organized itself in a fashion altogether different from that of the Græco-Roman churches. These latter churches were perfectly independent in their organization. The New Testament gives no hint that the apostles prescribed any form for the whole church. That the Twelve appointed James as "bishop" of Jerusalem is one of those unfounded statements which writers like Bishop Satterlee are fond of making, supposing their opinions to be facts. Eusebius says: The successors of James were *elected* "by the remaining *apostles* (not necessarily the Twelve) and *personal disciples* of the Lord with those who were *related to the Lord* according to the flesh," and Symeon " was put forward by all as the second in succession, being the cousin of the Lord " (Eccl. Hist. III, XI, 1, 2). That is, setting the apostles aside, the Jerusalem church, in a thoroughly eastern way, preserved the dynasty in the blood relations of Christ, until He should come again. The apostles may have agreed to this, but it was not their work. Each church did what any secular society can do, determined the simple matter as to who should be servant, be deacon or overseer in the church.

Whether the office-bearers in these churches were elected and formally installed or simply. *had* " preëminence " is not certain, but the latter is more probable. Those most diligent in labours, or the weightiest man, the natural patron of the society would be chief. Of this there is abundant evidence. It is much after this fashion that overseers are made in Church mission work.

Every local church, be it only three, has within itself all the power and right necessary for the performance of the duties of the whole Church. There is no Church function which three members of Christ's body cannot fulfill, because there is present the Father, the Son, the Holy Ghost. This was the true doctrine of the early Church, repeatedly affirmed.

Every local church has all the power of the whole Church. To this thought the early Church clung. The local church has been robbed of its right by a monarchical episcopacy. Christ's word, that He was

where two or three of His disciples met, and the
words in Hebrews, that believers are surrounded by a
great crowd of witnesses, found echo in such words
as that of Victor of Rome, that the Christian was to
place his money on the Lord's table, Christ being
present, angels watching and martyrs witnessing ; and
Origen said: angelic powers are present, the Lord
and Saviour Himself and the spirits of the saints, in
the assemblies of the faithful. Tertullian expresses
the idea (" Chastity," c. vii.) : " Accordingly, where
there is no joint session of the ecclesiastical order you
offer, baptize and are priest alone for yourself, for
where three are there is The Church, although they be
laity." He repeats this idea many times.

When Moberly asks whether the ministry comes
from beneath or above, here is the answer. It comes
truly from above, through the members of The Church ;
they are the source whence comes authority to any
to minister and not from any previously existing set of
officers. Moberly and the high-churchman put the
members of The Church below and officers on top.
The reverse of this is the Christian order.

As the water which flows in some mighty river to
the great sea, comes from the ten thousand rivulets
which are fed by the rains from heaven, so the authority and power of The Church comes not from a
few set channels, but from the spirit of God in the
myriads of Christians. As in the state, the divine
right of kings has perished and the divine right of the
people is restored, so may the divine right of lordship
in The Church perish forever !

Authority to rule resides *in The Church* itself. It may be delegated by The Church to a few but never so as to lose its own supreme authority. Christ gave His spirit to His Church. *The Church, not the set ministry,* is His body. The Church originally exercised that right, which no apostle ever usurped though he may have guided it, in local churches. Even though in the book of the Acts the author gives special prominence to the apostles, yet their preëminence was not dictatorial, and not so much due to being apostles as being prophets. This is certainly correct.

Any church has a right and authority to determine its own ministry, as protestant churches did at the Reformation, as the Methodist church did in the eighteenth century. This right pertains to Christians associated together.

The apostles themselves, in the larger use of that word which prevailed in the New Testament times and later, were born of the Spirit which was in The Church. Paul does not separate apostles from the prophets and teachers and the helps and tongue-gifted ones. They are *not over The Church.* They are *of* the church. Their gifts are not bestowed upon them in any other way than that whereby the humblest believer is endowed.

The mightiest oak in a forest has the same mother earth as the blade of grass and the same vital nature is in both. The mightiest apostle, as Paul, and the humblest servant in The Church, both alike derive their position from the Spirit which is in The Church. Out of The Church arise the Pauls and Bernards and

Luthers and Zaviers and Calvins and Wesleys and Jesus Himself. The Church can do no more than recognize the fact that God has "set them in The Church."

If a local church were a separate atom, a mere isolated unit, it would have no power to recognize any as ministers in The Church, but as it has the presence of Christ, as the whole Church is potentially there, it can act in the name of *the* Church, so far as it is spiritually a manifestation of The Church.

Thus the churches did in apostolic times. They accepted some as apostles, some as teachers.

It is constantly said, as a final and unanswerable argument by high-churchmen, "no man can make himself a Christian minister" (Mason: "Eccles. Unity," 1896, p. 92). Again he asks, "Who has authority to give sacramental bread?"

The answer is very simple: No man makes himself a Christian minister. It is God who does that, and He alone, by the gift of the Holy Spirit. No church can make a man a minister. The Roman, Anglican, Greek, and all the Oriental catholic officials combined cannot do that. All these can do is recognize and consecrate this spiritually gifted one. The form of his ordination, indeed the ordination itself, is a secondary matter, not a primary matter.

"The authority to give the sacramental bread" belongs to whomsoever any church appoints. Each church itself, and this does not mean merely a part of a church called a hierarchy, must in the most expedient fashion, set apart its official servants.

In Corinthians (1, 16 : 15), it is said that: " Stephanos and his followers had put themselves into the ministry to the saints," and Paul tells this church to submit themselves to such. And a later word in Clement (Cor. 38) gives the same command to be in subjection to others *as a gift is bestowed.* In the early church a *gift*, a charism, determined office or service. To secure order, Paul recognized one law, charity, love, so he puts 1 Cor. 13, between 12 and 14. This will hinder any schism. Paul relied on this (1 Cor. 12 : 25). He relied on the presence of Christ and the Spirit in the church. Therefore he gave no attention to officials, to rulers. The only authority was the word of God. (See Sohm, p. 28 ff.)

But this was the ideal. Human nature required regulation. Hence naturally and rightly, out of the " gifted " ones came officers who by reason of service, were also rulers.

The organization of a local church was through the permanency given to certain functions as most necessary for the life of the society. The functions which first became permanent were those pertaining to the distribution of alms and the care of the material interests of the community. The spiritual care of a congregation remained longer unsettled because there continued to be in every congregation those whose gifts enabled them to teach. But Acts 6 shows that the material interests first required regulation. It was so everywhere. Hence there were deacons in the Græco-Roman churches, and as the church work broadened, the episcopoi, in a church before there was

any settled teacher or pastor.   In the second century,
as the Didache shows, the wandering apostle, or
prophet, took precedence over the bishop or pastor
in a local church.   But, soon as the prophetic ministry waned, the leader of a church, the chief bishop, or
chief elder, would attend to the pastoral work.   Even
as early as 1 Timothy some of the local elders are to
be accounted worthy of special honour because they
labour in the Word as well as in the local affairs.
Thus there arose most naturally the threefold ministry, the deacons, the bishops (that is the presbyters)
and the chief of the presbyters labouring in the Word
called the bishop or pastor.   That he was called
bishop rather than presbyter when he reached his ele-
vation was due to the fact that the episcopal function
of the elder was regarded as the especial duty of the
elder.   He *was* an elder, but his *duty* was episcopal,
hence his title was that of bishop.   As a distinction
arose, the name bishop took precedence.

It may be regarded as the divine intention that the
gifts which God has bestowed upon Christians are to
be exercised, one with due reference to another, that
order is to prevail, and that efficiency is to be secured.

In every state of society, there are ranks and orders
of public service.   It must be so in a church.   Paul
defines this in the Ephesian letter; the end of all gifts
is the perfection of The Whole Church, which includes
a church.

The division of duties, the order of services, is voluntarily recognized by the Christians of a church,
large or small.   It is for well-being.   It is not, in any

form, essential to the being of a church. It is quite conceivable that Christians may continue as a church without any organization, simply united by their faith in God, their hope of the Kingdom and their love in the Holy Spirit.

This is, indeed an ideal church. And, organization with government is the temporary necessity of an imperfect state of things.

As there is " no temple " in heaven, so the perfect Christian Church is without external forms of organization. It is a perfect family of God. The Father of the family though absent from sight is spiritually present in all the members of the family. " Of whom every family is named."

XVII

IE FUTURE OF THE CHURCH AND THE CHURCHES

---

to Him be glory in the Church, by Christ Jesus, throughout all orld without end. Amen."—EPH. 3 : 21.

Church has a past, present, future.

: misconception as to Invisible Church.

invisible past ; the perfected saints.

: future of the imperfect, secular, church.

: Church of Christ : assured triumph.

: churches, representations.

: future of The Church not identical with that of a 1 or the churches.

: Church in the Wilderness.

nsitional periods involving decay of the old.

: Churches are mortal.

ional, local and secular elements.

: North-African churches.

: Oriental churches.

: British churches.

: Donatist.

ntanism.

: surviving catholic churches.

: mortality of the Roman Catholic Church.

: secularized.

: national.

The temporal element.
Elements of clay in this image.
Hostile forces at work in many nations.
America the hope of Roman Catholicism.
Americanism.
The Orthodox (Greek) Catholic Church.
Dependent on Russia.
The Anglican Church.
Not even the church of the Empire.
The Lutheran Church.
The Reformed Churches.
The Baptist Church.
The Presbyterian Church.
Calvinism.
No one church can become the exclusive church.
The True Church not necessarily perfect.
The Church interested in the churches.
Are the churches failures?
The widening breach between the churches and the age.
The age at fault as well as the churches.
The worth of The Church not staked on one church.
The Mission of the churches.
Godward, manward, selfward.
The gravest criticism : worship.
The work of a church : social.
The cultivation of character.
The triumph of The Church on earth must wait till
    unity comes.
Churches must agree.
What the churches must be and do.
Christ, the sacrificial saviour.

XVII

THE FUTURE OF THE CHURCH AND THE CHURCHES

WHEN we speak of the future of The Church we must remember that The Church is the existence form of the Christian religion.

The Church, as an entirety, has its existence in the past as well as in the present. The past of The Church is not extinct, but lives in the heavenly world. There is danger of confusion, if we use the phrases, the invisible and the visible church, because this leads to the idea that there is a visible church, which existing in a distinct and determined form is The True Church.

It is this error which more than any other, has led to the identification of The Church with a church. The Church, past, present and future, is one. There can be but one Church since Jesus Christ, the one head of The Church can have but one body. The Church may, therefore, be spoken of as having an invisible part. Thus, in Hebrews (12 : 23), we read that the " panegyric and ecclesia of the first-born, which are written in heaven " (the whole Church), has a part which is designated as " the spirits of the perfected righteous."

Of the Whole Church, part are already perfected.

Therefore, when we speak of the future of The Church we are referring to the manifestation of The

269

Church, which is still in the stage of imperfection upon
this earth.

The Church, as we have seen, has its manifestation
in the churches.

The *Whole* Church is The Church of Jesus Christ
since He is her only head and Redeemer.   She is His
bride.

Of this Church Jesus spoke when He said : " Thine
they were and Thou gavest them Me" (John 17 : 6).

Concerning this Church, Jesus said: " On this rock
I will build (*not found*, as Bengel well notes) My
Church, and the gates of hades shall not prevail against
it."

By which is meant not merely that The Church is
unconquerable by evil forces, but that all the power
of darkness shall be unable to resist its triumphant
march to victory.

In this sense, the angel on the white horse, who
went forth conquering and to conquer (Rev. 6 : 2),
symbolizes The Church.

Without the final triumph of The Church, the triumph of Jesus Christ is meaningless.   The glory and
supremacy of The Church is not to be realized in the
glory of any one at present existing church, since, as
we have seen, there is no one church which is The
Church.

Nor does this supremacy pertain to any class of
churches, whether called catholic or evangelic.

Nor, further, does it mean that all the existing
churches shall, as such, reach the glory form.

The churches do not constitute The Church (as Hort

suggests), *but these represent The Church*, in distinct forms of organization.

The Church which comes to manifestation in the churches, names, as we have seen, all the children of God who are perfected and also those who may be as yet imperfected on this earth. Christians form churches, and these churches again beget, by means of the Word, other Christians and other churches. The future of The Church is therefore not inseparably involved in the prosperity of any church, nor indeed of all the present churches. The Church in the Wilderness (Acts 7 : 38) of which Moses was the prophet and servant (Heb. 3 : 5) was to pass away. This passing away of Israel was a cause of alarm. It seemed the death of The Church of God.

But this transition did not involve the death of The Church, nor even the dimness of her glory. "The glory of the latter house shall be greater than the former" (Hag. 2 : 9). The passing away of the earlier form prepared the way, in the providence of God, for a new Israel, more worthy of the Spirit of God (Rom. 11). The old wine-bags may not answer for the new wine which comes with the new vintage of the Spirit of God.

Therefore, The Church passes not away even though the most magnificent of churches lose their beauty and power. We are not alarmed when some ark of God falls into the hands of the Philistines.

History furnishes us with facts which tell not only of the possibility but the actuality of the destruction of churches. All churches have in them elements

which may cause their ruin as churches. In every
church there are time elements, and elements of place
and race.

No church is a purely spiritual or eternal fact.

The seven churches of Asia are but samples of all
churches. They contain ingredients which cause the
Spirit to send His warnings (Rev. 2 and 3). There is
an awful liability, lest the love perish, lest purity pass
away, lest the light go out in darkness.

When any church is so identified with the peculi-
arities of a nation or an age that these dominate its
eternal and universal elements, such a church must
pass away or share the fate of the nation or the age.

A church may share the fate of the people or nation
with which it is identified. The most prosperous field
of The Church was North Africa. The Church at
Alexandria exceeded in power and glory that of Rome
or Antioch. Yet Augustine, from his death-chamber,
looked out on the advancing hordes of the Vandals
which made desert the places which had flourished
like the very garden in Eden. And with the secular,
went the religious strength and beauty.

And, what the Barbarians left was consumed by the
Moslem. Was it possible that if these churches had
been less zealous in persecuting one another, less
zealous in the differentiation of subtle doctrines, and
more zealous in prosecuting the work Jesus gave His
disciples; to preach and teach His gospel, that even
the Vandals had been turned aside; and there had
been no occasion for a Mohammed to teach Arabia a
better way of serving God? Who can say?

The churches which had extended their influence far away, and touched India and China and later Japan with something of the gospel, were themselves reduced to insignificant proportion through the overwhelming incursions of Tartar hordes, and the irresistible onslaught of Islam.

The churches in Persia and Syria and Abyssinia and in Asia Minor have dwindled during the centuries to mere shadows of their greatest power; partly through persecution, partly through their too close alliance with the age-spirit. They displayed more zeal in controversy with one another than in the conversion of the heathen and had more interest in dogmatic trifles and subtleties than in the weighty matters of Christian faith and love.

The fate of the British churches was more lamentable, since these had manifested to a rare degree the Christian spirit. Nevertheless these passed away, partly through the fate of wars, and partly through absorption in the greater church with its seat at Rome. The Donatist churches were either destroyed by their catholic antagonists, or were involved in the common calamities which overtook all North Africa.

Montanism, after a desperate struggle with catholicism, passed away; though not before it had given evidence of spiritual power, even if also of an unregulated enthusiasm.

From this hasty sketch it is apparent that *churches are mortal*, that *even catholic churches* do not bear a charmed life. Catholicism neither proved a bond of union, nor did it protect the weaker church from the aggression of more powerful rivals.

It is claimed by the surviving catholic churches that they rightly assume the title of The Church because they have survived so many vicissitudes during the centuries. We have considered this claim elsewhere. We now look at the matter from a different point of view; inasmuch as we affirm the mortality of these churches because they contain elements which are national, temporal, local.

It needs but to be stated to be believed, that so far as the two greatest of the catholic churches are concerned, these owe their persistence to their association with great empires.

How self-evident it is, that had not Rome and Constantinople been the mightiest of cities, then the churches which now rule such a wide domain from these same cities would have held a lower place.

If Carthage or Alexandria had proved mightier than Rome, then the fancied primacy of Peter would not have made the Roman church supreme.

If it be said that it was the fact that Rome was, and was destined to remain, the imperial city of the world that caused the Apostles Paul and Peter to set up there the Christian dominion; even this partial truth does not do away with the fact that it was this secular, imperial power which gave the Roman church its preëminence.

History leaves no doubt about the fact that this church contains perishable elements. Despite its claim of universality it is, in its spirit, localized. To this day it is essentially an Italian organization. The Latin blood fills its veins and the spirit of imperial Rome dictates its policy and its politics.

It is vast, imposing and has the grandeur of great force ; yet its force and beauty are largely secular. It is a world-power. It has succumbed to the temptation presented to Jesus, to bow down to evil that it might possess the Kingdoms of this world ; it has allied itself to physical force.

The endurance and the power of this organization are not due merely to the fact that it is a church, but that it is a world-kingdom claiming temporal power.

Affecting its permanency, in its present form, is the fact that it has been a *national church*, the church of one Empire.

The so-called Holy Roman Empire, which breathed its last just a century ago, furnished the field, as it furnished the resources, of this church. It is a Latin church, using that language. The Germans never really accepted its rule. Even the Franks, who became Latinized, have felt uneasy under its yoke, and their most recent revolt is familiar history. Only the Celts, of non-Latin peoples, have accepted it with enthusiasm, and Ireland and Brittany have hardly enjoyed the expected blessings.

The *temporal element* characterizes it strongly. It has immured itself behind ages of ignorance and fettered itself to its dogmatic errors by its announcement of its infallibility !

Science and philosophy since the days of Des Cartes and Galileo have now pleaded, now thundered, at the doors of the Inquisition, but the temporal element, the spirit of past ages, was too strong, and this church still denounces what is recognized truth, and resists those in its own ranks who would lead it to the truth which alone makes freedom.

How long must it be that men of science shall look down on its dogmatic position with mingled pity and contempt?

Not, of course, that this is the only church which has this temporal element of error, but this church is of all the most egregious.

For these reasons, because of these elements of clay which impoverish the element of gold, it must be admitted that even the Roman Catholic church, as it now exists, is like other catholic churches, mortal, even though it be so vast as to give but slow evidence of its perishability.

The signs of the times indicate the working of forces within and without it which must either make it a new and more glorious church or else bear it away to the grave. Almost an exile from France, regarded with mingled contempt and fear even in Italy, coldly welcomed in Rome itself, the object of popular antipathy in Spain, long so loyal, it has to turn to the Americas for the signs of hope on its dark horizon.

That the fate of this church will be settled in the United States of America seems almost sure.

But, from America also comes to Rome the alarming shadow of " Americanism." If the fate of the Roman church is settled in this free land, it means that the old Roman church will become a new, another church; or else that, as some have feared, freedom shall perish in the triumph of Rome.

The Orthodox (Greek) church is a mighty church, yet that it shall be The Church of the future is a dream which only Russian or Greek priests can cherish, if even they.

Only were Russia to be the one great world power could this church become the only, one, manifestation of The Church.   The prospect that Russia will attain the reach of her ambitions is almost beyond possibility. Inasmuch as the Greek church is so involved in the prosperity of the Russian Empire, it must share its vicissitudes.

True, it is more than a national church, yet so large a portion of it is national that it cannot ever expect to be The Church of the human race.

The Anglican church is not even the church of all the English, and circumstances do not indicate that it is likely to become the one church of the British Empire.   It must cease to be what it now is before even that is possible.   It is, as a national church, rendered incapable of being The One Church.   When Henry VIII repudiated the rule of Rome it was chiefly that he might be the independent head of the state church. Thus it is that the King of England is head of the " Established Church of England."

When we pass to the consideration of the protestant or evangelic churches, there is no one which is sufficiently free from the elements of time, locality, and nationality to become in its present form the sole representative of The Church.

The Lutheran church is, as its name implies, a church which perpetuates certain phrases of the Christion religion which are more or less exactly associated with this great German reformer.

The Lutheran Church, however, is not merely a church born of an epoch, it is further disqualified by the fact that it is almost entirely the church of one people, and has spread but little beyond it.

The other churches of the Reformation likewise represent elements that are local or temporal or racial, which disqualify them as candidates for The One Church.

A church which insists that all Christians must be immersed after a personal confession of faith may, although it is exceedingly improbable, bring all other Christians either to the positive acceptance of this doctrine, or the passive acquiescence in it. Yet it may be regarded as equally certain, that other churches will insist on the adoption of their own pet belief or practice, and only accept that of another church through exchange or compromise.

That the *Calvinistic churches* will ever induce all other churches to accept Calvinism is beyond expectation except on the part of a few ardent supporters of these articles of belief, and this possibility, which has three centuries against it, has been weakened in recent years by the practical abandonment of Calvinism by the Presbyterian churches in Scotland and by the Presbyterian church in the United States of America. This altogether apart from the truth in these doctrines.

It would be superfluous to examine the possibilities of other churches, whose doctrines include either much more or much less than that which must characterize The True Church.

It is a conclusion which few will dispute, that while it is possible that many churches may contribute some element to some one almost universal and final church which shall be the best obtainable representation of The True Church because including nearly all the living children of God, yet no one church existing to-day but contains so much that is perishable, so much that is local or temporal or temperamental, as to be destined to change of form, change of creed, change of worship. As time changes, temperaments alter, and a church passes from one locality to another, so must it undergo alteration.

The rise of new churches in foreign lands is to be hoped for.

Of no church, catholic or evangelic, can it be said that its form of government, its mode of worship, its doctrine is so fixed and eternal that it is the one church to which all others must come: Christ is larger, grander than any or all the churches, and The True Church is the Bride of Christ.

To the foregoing it is possible that some one may object, that the ideal or perfect Church is not identical with The True Church; that The Church may be *true, but not ideal.* This is correct enough; but, it is only The True Church which can become the ideal Church and that church alone which can become the ideal

Church without alteration of that which characterizes it, can be the True Church.

Therefore, when we have shown that a church must change, as the Roman Catholic church, its claim to infallibility, for example; or a Presbyterian church its presbytery; such a church is not the *imperfect True Church*, but is not *The True Church at all;* it is merely a church.

It would be a false inference from the foregoing to conclude The Church is not interested in the fate of the churches.

The future of The Church though *not identical* with that of any one church nor indeed of all churches, is nevertheless involved in that of the Churches. The members of The Church are the members of the churches.

The failure of churches means the failure, to some extent, of their members, both as to what they are and what they do.

Therefore *interest in the True Church requires that we be interested in all the churches*, not merely in our own.

There are many who regard the churches as failures. Statements to this effect are current and popular.

Many friends of the Christian religion view the situation with alarm, while there is corresponding exultation among its enemies. We have already indicated reasons for the hope that the seeming failure of the churches may be but transitional movements whereby the Christian religion and therefore The Church is actually benefited.

But, the churches can never afford to be indifferent to their own condition.   Unless the churches realize their mission, The Church suffers through loss both of members and through their imperfection.   The Church is like the nation and the states, in their mutual relationship.

Therefore one cannot help feeling alarmed at the appalling gap which seems to be widening between the churches and the so-called masses on the one side and the classes of cultured and scientific on the other.

It may be easy to exaggerate this fact and to become unduly despondent.

To find fault with the churches as solely responsible is quite customary.   The writer is persuaded that the churches are much less at fault than is commonly supposed.   The age is at fault more than the churches.

It is out of our purpose to enter into a discussion of all the accusations brought against the churches.   For the most part, these are invented in order to serve as excuses for the neglect of religion, and for the desire to be independent of the government of God.   If some churches are unchristian, all are not, and there should be a willingness to recognize this fact.

If the worth of The Church was staked on some one of the churches, then there might be reason in bringing an accusation against The Church.   But, The Church, as we have seen, is more than the mightiest of churches.

In considering the future of The Church we should remind ourselves of *the mission of The Church*, that the churches may be tested thereby.

Paul says : " Unto Him be glory in The Church by

Christ Jesus" (Eph. 3 : 21); and again: "That the manifold wisdom of God might be known through The Church" (Eph. 3 : 10). In the fourth chapter of this letter Paul gives quite fully the mission and duty of The Church.

This duty is threefold:

> Godward
> Manward
> Selfward.

That is, upward, outward, inward.

This threefold mission involves the Trinity: Upward to the Father: Manward, as the Son; Inward, by the Spirit.

The first duty is worship, the second is work, the third is edification.

These three are inseparable: to neglect one, is to neglect all.

Worship must have the elements which Jesus Christ named sincerity, spirituality (John 4 : 24).

The churches which worship God most sincerely and spiritually will draw closely to one another, because such worship characterizes The True Church.

All true Christians do so worship God, or desire to.

The gravest criticism to be passed on churches of to-day is that they do not so worship God.

There is lack of sincerity: there is lack of the Spirit of God.

The cry of the day is for social effort. No objection can be made to this demand, unless it take the churches away from their first duty, which is Godward.

It is in the matter of worship, that most churches are defective.

But the churches must be working organizations, as Jesus Christ wrought for man.

There is much misunderstanding concerning the nature of this work.   Jesus Christ gives the examples of Christian and Church work: " Even as the Son of Man came not to be ministered unto but to minister." " As My Father hath sent Me, so send I you."

The ministry of Jesus Christ is *primarily* and finally a *work to save man:* that is, to make man's life a divine life; to make man perfect in the likeness of God.

If a church becomes a mere eleemosynary institution it is in danger of separation from The True Church.

It may be necessary for a church to resist the demands made upon it, as Jesus Christ did, to be a divider of earthly goods.   He declined to make stones, bread.   He refused to be a bread-king.

This does not mean that a church shall not exercise charity and demand justice.   The Christian and a church can have no higher law : do justly, love mercy, and walk humbly with God (Micah 6 : 8).

The Christian's law is " bear one another's burdens " (Gal. 6 : 2).

But, the duty of love to a fellow man is not fully performed unless the life, the soul of man, is saved from the worship of mammon.

The Christian's duty to his fellow man, and therefore the work of a church, is that he be made a man of faith and hope and love, in the spirit of Jesus Christ.

The churches have, also, a duty selfward, in the cultivation of Christian character in all the members of a church.

Paul emphasized this constantly: "till we all come in the unity of the faith unto a perfect man" (Eph. 4 : 13).

Peter exhorts: "grow in grace and in the knowledge of Jesus Christ" (2 Pet. 3 : 18).

The triumph of The Church on earth must, historically, wait until the churches agree in their work for man's redemption, for the true worship of God, and the perfection of the Christian character.

The churches must furnish mankind with true fellowship with God, through Jesus Christ. The churches, if they would do God's work, if they desire the triumph of The Church, must not "be conformed to this world, but transformed" and transforming.

The churches do not need to adapt themselves to the age, so much as to adapt the age and themselves to the golden age of the Kingdom of God.

The churches must, indeed, hear the demands of the times, but above all to heed and teach the commands of God, of Jesus Christ.

The churches must offer to mankind more than a new moral code, more than a social brotherhood on secular lines, more than better wages and better times. The churches, if the Church of Christ is to triumph, must present to man the forgiveness of sins, reconciliation with God, and a renewed nature capable of enjoying God and His works both in this life and the life to come.

The churches must meet the needs of man's intelligence, so far as possible in conformity with God's truth, in their creeds; they must, so far as it be possible in Spirit and sincerity, in worship meet the demands of the heart, and the æsthetic sense. But, first of all, the *churches must present and represent the Christ who sacrificed Himself for man's redemption. This and This alone will secure the triumph of The Church.*

The trials and the triumph of The Church of God is the theme of the Sacred Scriptures.

There is a striking unity of thought in the earliest and in the latest chapters of our Bible.

" I will put enmity between thee and the woman, between thy seed and her seed; it shall bruise thy head and thou shalt bruise his heel" (Gen. 3: 15).

This has been, is to be, the history of The Church, " the seed of the woman," which is also the seed of God.

In the twelfth chapter of the Revelation we have the vivid vision granted unto St. John who sees the fuller story of this struggle anticipated in Genesis.

Secluded on the isle of Patmos, the holy seer has a revelation which shows " the woman clothed with the sun, the moon under her feet and upon her head a crown of twelve stars " (Rev. 12: 1).

The seed of the woman is born amid great tribulation. The serpent is ready to devour it up. The first-born of the woman, " who was to rule all nations with a rod of iron," " was caught up unto God, and to His throne." So Jesus, the seed (Gal. 4: 4; 3: 16), was caught up into heaven.

Jesus Christ is both son and lord of The Church, as He is David's son and lord.

Though her son and lord is caught away, yet the woman is left to endure the persecution of the evil one.

"And the woman fled into the wilderness." The persecution of the woman is the persecution of The Church. Then "the earth helped the woman." The Church emerges from obscurity; the days of greatest trial are over when "the time and times and half-time" are passed, when in the middle of the fourth century, The Church becomes the chosen ally of the Empire. While there came from this alliance of The Church with the material resources of the Empire much that tended to diminish the pure lustre of The Church, yet the union was necessary in the divine providence in order that the earth itself might feel the vitalizing force of The Church.

In this vision, the woman and "the remnant of her seed" represent The Church and her children "which kept the commandments of God and have the testimony of Jesus Christ" (Rev. 12 : 17).

The ages past have been ages of conflict, often ages of anguish. The serpent has bruised the heel of the seed of the woman (Gen. 3: 15).

At times it has seemed as though "the great dragon, that old serpent, called the devil and Satan," symbolizing the powers of darkness would prevail over the woman and her seed.

But The Church has never lost all her seed; her life has never become extinct. Those who keep the commandments of God have never failed from among men.

The Church has become the mother of a vast army of those who call Jesus their elder brother, the first-born.

Time would fail to tell of them, and their deeds, who, both in ancient and modern times, have through faith subdued kingdoms, wrought righteousness, obtained promises, stopped the mouths of lions, quenched the violence of fire, out of weakness were made strong, waxed valiant in fight, turned to flight the armies of the aliens.

Time would fail to tell of these individual victors who have contributed to the triumph of The Church who faced earthly powers without fear, and braved the violence of nature, calmly confronted the fury of mobs and trembled not at the wrath of the rulers of men; as Polycarp who went unflinching to the fire and whose courage made it useless to bind him amid the flames; as Ignatius, who embraced martyrdom as the sweetest of brides and longed that his body might be bread to the wild beasts that his spirit might the better praise God; as Blandina, who endured the cruelest of tortures without wavering; as Francis of Assisi, who preached the beautiful gospel of poverty and peace and would undergo the ordeal of fire that he might convert the Saracen ruler; as Raymond Lull, who carried the gospel among the unbelieving followers of the false prophet; as Huss, who died at the stake rather than deny the truth he had fearlessly proclaimed, as Luther and Zwingli and Calvin and Knox who, true children of The True Church, sought to release their mother from the fatal embraces of the unregenerated world. Time would fail to tell of such as Morrison, of Judson, of Henry Martyn and Pattison and Mackay and the martyrs of

China and the ten thousand times ten thousand to whom The True Church has been mother, bringing them into fellowship with the Eternal Son.

The vision of John assures us that The True Church and all her children shall at the last be gathered together. The apocalypse shows us the heavenly city crowded with angels; its walls resound with acclamations; at its gates are cherubim and seraphim; harpers are sounding their harps, seraphic voices are singing melodious harmony, as the noise of many waters fills the air, the hallelujahs ascend unto God and unto His Son as the children of lesser degree, who have kept the faith of Christ, who have cherished the hope of the Kingdom of God the Father, who have preserved the love of the Holy Ghost, advance to the city of the Great King. The Church comes; fair as the morn, clear as the sun, terrible as an army with banners. The ransomed of the Lord come to Zion with songs and everlasting joy, to be welcomed by the Captain of their salvation, to take blissful possession of the new heaven and the new earth wherein dwelleth righteousness.

Thus the Sacred Scriptures foresee the triumph of The Church. And the churches on earth pray, and work as they pray!

Our Father which art in heaven,
Hallowed be Thy name;
Thy kingdom come,
Thy will be done,
On earth, as in heaven
Give us this day our daily bread,

Forgive us our debts as we forgive our debtors
Lead us not into temptation
But deliver us from evil
For Thine is the kingdom and the power and the glory, forever. *Amen.*

APPENDIX

THE CHURCH AS INVISIBLE AND VISIBLE

THAT in some sense The Church is invisible is not only taught by protestants, but also by catholics.

That protestants taught two churches, as Bellarmine urged, is not strictly true, even though language might seem to yield this result, and even though some protestants have seemed so to do. This is not, however, a necessary protestant position. It is not the protestant who teaches two churches, one invisible and the other visible,—it is the catholic who does so. The protestant teaches that the One Church has an invisibility, since no man can see it perfectly. Visible or institutional Christianity is *not The* Church, it is a part of, a manifestation of The Church.

The catholic really teaches two churches, one visible, the other invisible, because he calls *a* church, *The* Church, and yet says that there is another church within it which is the real bona fide Church.

Writing from the Anglican-catholic viewpoint, Durell says : " The Church has a spiritual existence apart from its outward or institutional form. We may regard as universal the idea that the Church is not merely the company of the faithful, but has also a mystical existence as the sphere of grace into which the faithful are gathered.

" The definite distinction which we find both in Hermas and the Pseudo-Clement, between the institutional church and the spiritual church is an expression of the doctrine that though the members of the *outward* church have the way of salvation open to them, it depends on their own efforts whether they reach the goal" ("The Historic Church," p. 301).

According to this the organized Church is a probationary institution. And this is the catholic notion. Hooper taught this difference between The True Church and The Church as man sees it. So also does Hooker, and Field.

The position of Darwell Stone ("The Christian Church") is contradicted by the Articles of Religion which use the phrase "visible church," plainly teaching as Calvin taught, that there is an invisibility about The True Church.

Augustine distinguishes: "Some are in such sort in the house of God that they also *are* the house of God, and some are so in the house of God that they pertain not to the frame and fabric of it."

If this visible "frame" is *The Church*, then we have here two churches, an inner church and an outer. Only by admitting that *a* church, which man sees is not *The* Church, but only a part of, a local manifestation of The Church, which takes on necessarily local and temporal features, can we escape the dualism of the catholic church notion.

The Anglicans can still less claim that the visible association of Christians is The Church, because these admit that the Roman Catholic Church is, to use their constant language, "a *part* of The Church."

Therefore the Roman Church, by their confession, is not The Church, nor is the Anglican, nor is the Greek. These are only *manifestations* of The Church, and there are others.

Only when we admit that churches are only partial manifestations of the True Church, can we avoid the incredible "two Church" notion. We cannot call any church The

Church, and yet say that The Church is more than, or other than this which is so called.

If the Anglican Church is not coextensive with The Church, it *is not* The Church. The same holds true of the Greek and the Roman Churches. That is, churches are manifestations of a larger reality which is alone The True Church, invisible in its totality, but so far manifest in the churches which contain members of The True Church.

The opinions of A. RITSCHL on this subject are of interest.

Ritschl had long occupied himself with the notion of The Church. As Oman says, it is the central idea of his theology. He wrote for a prize essay, " de ecclesiæ invisibilis notione," in his twentieth year. (See Leben, I, p.63.)

His latest opinion is given in his " Rechtfertigung," and in the " Unterricht."

Ritschl defines The Church as " those who believe in Christ, so far as they present their prayer to God the Father, or themselves to God as pleasing, through Christ."

The Kingdom he defines as " those who believe in Christ so far as they, regardless of race, etc., act out of love to one another " (Rechtf., III, p. 266, 2d Ed.).

For Ritschl, The Church is the fellowship (gemeinschaft) which Christ established to realize the purpose of God in the forgiveness of sins. Every member of this community has the right to announce the justifying grace of God, but especially the official representatives of the Church. Along with these human organs, the sacraments are bearers of the grace of God, together with the word of the gospel (Rechtf., III, p. 103 ff.).

To Ritschl, and here he follows both Luther and Calvin, The Church, as the communion of saints, is the association within which the grace of God prevails.

Ritschl opposes to the assurance of forgiveness which the mystic has who relies on his personal experience, the word of the gospel which avails in The Church.

The Church is the communion of the saints which can never have the visibility of an institution. This is The True Church. And for the Apostles, Ritschl says, the Kingdom is the expression of the Christian hope, and The Church, the present institution for its realization (Rechtf., III, p. 266).

He says, that Augustine introduces the fatal notion that the Kingdom is The Church under the rule of the apostles and bishops.

In this catholic "Kingdom of God" Ritschl declares, righteousness consists in selfish usurpation and in the use of all means of deceit and violence (Rechtf., III, p. 267).

In 1859 Ritschl wrote for the *Studien und Kritiken* a criticism of Münchmeyer's opinion on The Church. He entitles his dissertation, " UEBER DIE BEGRIFFE : SICHTBARE UND UNSICHTBARE KIRCHE."

Ritschl says that Zwingli was the first to make use of the distinction between the visible and invisible Church. By which he must mean a distinction which made each adjective name a distinct Church.

For Zwingli, the invisible Church is the elect, only God sees this Church. The visible Church is all those who confess Christ, whether truly or not.

Concerning this notion, Ritschl goes on to note certain difficulties. For example, inasmuch as all those who really believe must likewise confess their faith, so the members of the invisible Church must become visible.

Also, an invisible Church such as Zwingli affirms as over against a visible Church, would exclude the possible relationship of its members one with another. It would be a circle without any circumference ; merely isolated points.

Zwingli is not consistent, because he now speaks of the Church as the true believers, and again as the elect. But all the elect may not at a given time be believers. And if they are believers, then they must be so far visible, since belief involves confession. And so, the invisible Church, is, in part at least, not invisible, but visible.

In distinction from the Zwinglian notion of the invisible and visible churches, Ritschl makes clear that Huss escapes the difficulties in which Zwingli involved himself.

Huss called The Church the totality of the elect ; past, present, and to come. The unity of The Church rested on predestination. In the present time this unity rests on faith and virtue (virtus), and love.

The Church is thus the body of Christ, though like the body, it contains what does not really belong to it.

Connected with The Church are children of the devil. The Church as seen by faith is the genuine church ; as seen by sight, it is imperfect. It is the same body as seen from two viewpoints (as from above or below the horizon).

The Church of the predestined is not yet a reality, except as it exists in the will of God. Yet the predestinated are in part a real Church, and visibly so, so far as it is " *in unitate fidei et virtutum et in unitate caritatis.*"

Therefore, with Huss the defined idea of The Church as the predestinated includes the visibility of this Church on earth. That one cannot discern the evil, makes The True Church an object of faith ; it is spiritually discerned. The Church is invisible only because our human judgment errs. That is, The Church is so far the realization of the divine idea, and is visible.

There is an unknowableness about The Church so far as

the membership of individuals is concerned. Faith sees
the perfect Church without spot or blemish, even though
there are in the Church those who belong to the "*ecclesiæ
diaboli.*"

The judgment of the world makes no distinction, but faith
does. Thus there are not two churches for us, a visible and
an invisible church. The Church is invisible only as The
Church seen by sight has elements which we cannot abstract.

Thus Huss did not dispute that the Papal church was an
excellent part of The Universal Church.

Ritschl contends that Luther follows the idea of Huss,
rather than the notion of Zwingli; and it is mainly his contention in his essay to show the superiority of Luther's concept over that of Zwingli and Calvin.

For Luther, The True Church, although invisible, *i. e.,*
an object of faith, has, however, certain signs from which
her presence may be certainly concluded. Luther is quoted
to this effect : "That the Church is the congregation or
assemblage of all those who live in right faith, love and
hope. And so that true Christendom is not a bodily association, but *a congregation of hearts in one faith.* So, although we may be bodily separated thousands of miles, so
long as each preaches and believes and hopes and loves and
lives like the other, we call this a spiritual congregation, and
the unity is a spiritual unity. And this alone is enough to
make a Christenheit. And without this spiritual unity, no
unity of state, or time, or person, or work, or whatever it
may be, can ever make a Christenheit. The Holy Church
is not bound to Rome, but is as broad as the world is, inasmuch as it is spiritually one in faith." [1]

Ritschl maintains that it is an error to suppose that
Luther, in distinguishing between the inner and outer

[1] The translation is abridged.

Christianity, maintains the Zwinglian notion of invisibility and visibility, because visibility *is* predicated by Luther of the so-called spiritual and inner Church.

The communion of saints by faith has an essential and necessary appearance, because the gospel and the sacraments, which are essential to the earthly existence of the spiritual Church, according to Luther, give it a measure of visibility.

So that The Church, even in the dogmatic sense, is not in itself invisible. And if Luther were to maintain this, he certainly would involve himself in contradiction.

When Luther speaks of the invisible Church, it is of The Church as the object of faith. He excludes the notion that The Church is essentially bound to some political form of it, as set forth, for example, in the Roman Church.

The Church is invisible only as over against a false notion of its visibility; that is, that The True Church is an object of carnal vision.

Luther did not underestimate the need of forms, which he called a moral need and a necessity for the continuance of the communion of saints on earth. This he maintained over against the Donatistic tendencies of the Anabaptists.

It was over against those who sought to purify the Church, that Luther maintained that The Church on earth must of necessity have in it more than the number of the elect. He says: "When we allow no weeds, we have no Church."

That is, Luther maintained The Church *on earth* could not by any human process be made perfectly pure; and the effort to make it perfectly pure would, as Christ taught, mean that in removing tares the wheat also would go with them.

So that Luther maintained that the effort to purify absolutely The Church would end by making it but a sect of the devil.   [This, of course, raises a very difficult question, as to discipline.]

In so doing Luther, however, does not accept the catholic definition of The Church.   The Church, *so far as it includes the weeds is not an object of faith, and this The True Church is.*   But he does regard The Church, so far as it is a political fellowship, as an object of practical interest and of moral obligation.   That is, The Church, as organized, even though it be imperfect as it is, has claim on all those who would be Christians.

He agrees with the Anabaptists, that the Church *as an object of faith* is a communion of saints, and not of saints and sinners.   But, this Church being an object of faith, could not be made as the Anabaptists wanted it, a visible reality.   That is, The Church which man knows on earth can never perfectly correspond with The Church which God knows.

For Melancthon, The Church is not so much a society of external things and rights, but is principally a society formed by faith and the Holy Spirit in the hearts of men. Yet this Church, nevertheless, has external notes, so that it is possible to know it, viz.: The pure doctrine of the gospel and the sacraments administered according to the gospel of Christ.

The Church is not like Plato's Republic, a mere conviction, it really exists as a communion of saints.   Its existence is not in a particular place, nor is it a particular people, nor does it necessarily require agreement of external ceremonies.   But it is universal so far as it embraces those scattered through all the earth, who are, nevertheless, bound together by common relationship to Jesus Christ.

This Church is pillar and ground of truth, because she holds to Christ as the foundation of salvation.   As a political organization, The Church embraces the unholy. The wicked are not members of The True Church. Thus Melancthon.

Ritschl criticises Melancthon for using the words "not alone," as though the Church were partly one, and partly the other, as though The Church exists in two distinct forms. He says Melancthon wavers here. He thinks that Melancthon errs when he maintains an objective difference between two churches, and when he speaks of duo corpora ecclesiæ; that is the ecclesia hypocritica and the ecclesia vera.

And elsewhere he speaks of The Church properly (proprie dicta) so-called, and The Church spoken of generally (large dicta).

Ritschl, while thus criticising Melancthon, inclines to the opinion that he did not really differ from Luther, but is careless in his expressions. So that in the main, Melancthon positively agrees with Luther's notion of The Church.

For them both, The Church so far as it is an object of faith, is the communion of saints, which through the divine force of the gospel and of the sacraments, is continually brought forth; and at the same time, with all these factors as visible marks, is recognized by faith.

The Church indeed has, moreover, also political marks, as appears in the contrast between ministers and congregation, and herein The Church has existence as a legal organization like the State. And in this organization even the children of the devil may have place.

There is a moral necessity for the believers that The Church should exist in this legal way. But as such she is not the object of faith. And so Luther speaks of The Church *proprie dicta* as having invisibility, while Melancthon predicates visibility of The Church only indirectly.

This does not indicate any contradiction between them both, only that Luther speaks of The Church from the apologetic point of view, but Melancthon from the dogmatic.

Later, according to Ritschl, Melancthon introduces also the *ministerium evangelii* as a mark of The Church, and includes all who confess. In this "ministerium" there is a suggestion of government which, Ritschl says, is a step towards catholicism, if it be made a necessary mark of The Church as seen by man on earth.

Luther had also gone in this direction, says Ritschl, when he makes one of the seven marks of the Church, the call of Church servants. But, both Luther and Melancthon here are not referring to The Church *as the object of faith, but to the empirically realized Church.* This he concludes from the fact that the injunction is given to those who stray and wander and join no Church, to join the Church most correctly formed—that is, the evangelical. (Here "church" names a politically organized association.)

That is, both Luther and Melancthon hold to this notion: The Church is the object of faith, which yet has visibility in the churches formed by the word and of the sacraments.

So Melancthon says in the last half of his *Loci*, "We do not imagine an invisible Church alone, but the eyes and mind see a company of the called, those who are profiting by the preaching of the gospel."

Ritschl criticises Calvin for seeming to make a too decided difference between the visible and invisible churches. Though he holds the ethical view of The Church as presented by Melancthon in his *Loci*, yet he is not so clear. With him also, The Church is a *moral* necessity. And as such The Church has its pastors and teachers, its word and sacraments, which are modes by which we come to God. This he calls the visible Church. And, while included in the confession "I believe in the Holy Catholic Church," yet this confession refers not alone to this visible Church, but to all the elect, including the past and the future.

It is a matter of faith, according to Calvin, because man cannot distinguish the true and the false. Yet this visible Church, according to Calvin, is our mother. This visible Church, however, includes also hypocrites and sinners. (Here Calvin becomes catholic.)

According to Ritschl, Calvin seems to suggest that the private individual, with his judgment test of love may distinguish the true from the false disciple, may know " who profess the same Christ with us by their confession of faith and example of life, and participation in the sacraments."

As Ritschl suggests, this judgment of love can easily become a judgment of lovelessness. Ritschl charges against Calvin that The Church is in *itself invisible*, and yet that Calvin recognizes signs whereby this invisible Church can be detected.

While Calvin thus gets into questionable opinions, yet Ritschl says that Calvin is following Luther and Melancthon in the words, " Wherever the Word of God is sincerely preached and heard, wherever the sacraments of Christ's institution are seen in administration, there without doubt The Church is to be found, because nowhere is it possible for these to be but that they bring forth fruit and prosper by the blessing of God."

According to this, invisibility does not in the true sense belong to the Church. Yet, according to Ritschl, Calvin does come into decided conflict with himself in speaking of this Church which is made up of true and false Christians, as the object of faith, for the Church of faith is only the ideal vision of the reality.

Ritschl's conclusion with regard to these views of the Reformers is that they lack discrimination. The Reformers recognize the political church; that is, the need of organization and the moral need that the communion of saints shall be a social community.

But Ritschl says that neither Luther nor Melancthon nor Calvin is conscious that he is here on moral, ethical grounds, and not on dogmatic grounds.

Ritschl says: "The Church is object of faith and of the knowledge based on faith, and as such is the communion of saints which is grounded and bound together by means of the divine factors of the gospel and the sacraments, and has its necessary marks in these, through which also it comes to manifestation.

"*The Church is therefore visible and perceptible for the kind of experience which alone is appropriate to her nature, viz.: faith.* With this thought of Luther's and Melancthon's, with which also Calvin involuntarily agrees, we decide against the intentional view of Zwingli and Calvin, that The Church is to be defined as in itself an *invisible* community of those whom God has elected to salvation.

"For this election is accomplished in reality only, according to Calvin, through these factors. And when Zwingli does not bring these factors as necessary into view, in order that he may let the heathen count as elect, and that he may reckon those who pertain to the future as belonging to The Church, so in part he overlooks the historical element in the divine counsel of election, and in part confuses the idea of The Church with the divine idea of the kingdom of God."

NOTES

Darwell Stone has written a valuable book entitled "The Christian Church," London, 1905, in which he presents the catholic concept of the Church. He follows the Augustinian notion that the Kingdom is the Church, and so represents the same school as Moberly, Liddon, and Gore. He combats Newman's conception that "Christianity came into the world as an idea rather than an institution." He constantly assumes the issue, "The Christian system has been embodied in a visible Church." "The history of religion involves a church." His fallacy is in assuming that *a* church is *the* Church. He, himself, admits that there are at least three churches. The identity of Church and Kingdom he finds in that baptism is the entrance to both (p. 36). For this statement there is no valid evidence. By baptism is secured public entrance into some manifestation of The Church, but into the Kingdom man comes through a new birth, and these are not necessarily the same.

IV

Henson, H. H., "Apostolic Christianity," London, 1898, says: "The Christian Church was literally the offspring of the synagogue" (p. 4). It is a "secession from the synagogue." "The autonomy of the ecclesia was subject to (1) the laws of Christ, (2) the moral law of the Old Testament, (3) Apostolic authority."

"The Apostolic Church was not congregational, nor presbyterial, nor episcopal."

"Paul's teaching precludes the existence of any visible centre of unity."

"On the whole view of the last four centuries non-episcopal Christianity has proved its power to stand the test proposed by our Lord. Its fruits are indisputable" (p. 302).

"The exclusive claims of types of ecclesiastical order constitute perhaps the most obdurate and general of such stumbling blocks" to the unity of the Spirit. "Most of these claims are certainly false, all are probably exaggerated, all may be found ultimately to be baseless" (p. 305).

V

Plitt, Hermann, "Gemeine Gottes," Gotha, 1859, says: "The Church is in essence ' spiritual, eternal, and rests on the union of its members with God and one another in Christ through faith and love ' " (s. 2).

Its "form is conditioned by human conditions of space and time."

The Church has its two sides, a visible and an invisible, a physical and a spiritual, but "*not that there are two distinct gemeinschaften* (communions)."

The inner communion, Plitt prefers to call " Kingdom," which he defines as " the invisible, though real, unity, in which all God's children are at home."

" Each church must confess that it is not the Kingdom, and yet must work that the Kingdom is in it " (s. 16).

" We have recognized a multitude of visible churches as divinely intended (Gottgewollt), inevitable and beneficial, and the duty of Christendom is not found in an artificial and forced unity, but in a spiritual unity of knowledge and love."

Charles Hodge says: (" Church Polity ") " If a body of professing Christians is organized in a certain way, it is a church, no matter whether it is as heretical and idolatrous as Rome, or as ignorant and superstitious as the Greeks and Abyssinians."

" The protestant doctrine which makes the profession of the true religion the only essential criterion of the Church is neither arbitrary nor optional. It is necessary and obligatory " (p. 139).

" People do not confer the office, but join in the exercise of a judgment whether a given person is called of God to be a minister."

John Brown (" Apostolic Succession "), says (p. 34) : " One universal church organization is hitherto unattained and unattainable. The bishop came through the cessation of charismatic gifts and the cessation of itinerant apostles, prophets and teachers " (pp. 219–221).

He says : " The Anglican claim is recent and modern, and is first urged as a counter-claim to presbyterianism " (p. 399).

He quotes Archbishop Tait :—" He could hardly imagine there were two bishops on the bench, or one clergyman in fifty, who would deny the validity of a Presbyterian clergyman solely on account of their wanting the imposition of episcopal hands."

To this, the *Church Quarterly Review* somewhat angrily replied :

" If the episcopate is unnecessary for valid ordination, the Church of England is guilty of no little tyranny, not to say schism, in her treatment of non-episcopal communities " (*Church Review*, October, 1885).

Dr. Brown's conclusion is :—" The Church is a divine society which is supernatural not because it is ruled by a heaven-ordained priesthood, but because the Spirit of God dwells in every member of the Church commonalty " (p. 444).

J. V. C. Durell says : " The one universal Church is represented in each place by the local church in that place " (" Historic Church," p. 302).

[This " one universal Church," however, is itself nowhere on earth fully manifested. It is not to be identified with any one church, be it Roman or Greek, or Anglican. Nor with all churches put together. These manifest this one Church, which is perfectly manifest alone to God, and exists as an eternal reality beyond its temporal manifestations.]

As to the relation of the Christian Church to the Church of the pre-Christian dispensation Richard Field, Dean of Gloucester (of whom Fuller spoke as " The Field the Lord hath blessed "), says: " Though the Church of the Old and New Testament be in essence the same, yet for that the state of the Church of the New Testament is in many respects far more glorious and excellent, the Fathers for the most part appropriate the name Christian to the multitude of believers since the coming of Christ " (See his " Five Books of The Church ").

Goldwin Smith has recently written concerning the Anglican church : " Laud, on the scaffold, declared that he 'had always lived in the Protestant Church of England.' "

" The king when crowned, has, till Edward VII taken a strong anti-catholic oath, and he is head of the Church."

" It is surely idle to deny that down to the rise of Tractarianism, sixty years ago, the Church of England and all its members considered themselves Protestant, called themselves Protestant."

" It seems impossible to deny, that legally and historically the national Church of England is Protestant."—*The Independent*, N. Y., September 2, 1907.

In " Our Churches and Why We Belong to Them," Webb–Peploe says : " The Church of England knows nothing of a sacrificing priesthood " (p. 364).

The possible *unity of churches* is differently viewed.

" It is strange that people do not see the futility of union on a governmental basis " (" Basis of True Christian Unity," Kettlewell).

Over against this, A. J. Mason says: (" Principles of Ecclesiastical Unity," p. 90) " Certainly it is a vain thing to endeavour to reunite christendom upon the basis of a recognized anarchy."

" Historically, the Church is an organization. The ministry is an important part, owing its inception to Jesus Christ Himself."

Dr. Mason's position simply is, You must come in to us, if there is to be church unity. He insists, as the Anglican catholics always do, on the sentence which nobody disputes, " No man can make himself a Christian minister." As we have already said, it is God alone who can make a minister, and each church recognizes its ministers according to its own best judgment.

Mason says further: " The Apostolic ministry can only be derived from the transmission from those who, as Timothy and Titus, have thus been solemnly entrusted therewith " (p. 93).

It would be very interesting to have Dr. Mason show the connection between his ordination and that of Timothy and Titus.

He further says: " To enter into communion with the protestant churches would bar the way to any reunion with the as yet unreformed churches of christendom " (p. 102).

Yet, Dr. Mason admits all the great schisms of antiquity except perhaps the Montanist, were organized by men in undoubted orders. He frankly says (p. 107), " Rome is the hole of the pit when spiritually we were digged."

And again, " The English Church is the daughter of Rome. The primacy of Rome is divine in the larger sense in which history reveals the divine will " (p. 109).

Reville (" Les Origines," p. 151), " It is the lamentable prejudice of the unity of primitive Christianity which has induced the theologians to seek a uniformity in the external constitution of the first churches." " Episcopate, no more than any other ecclesiastical function, is not of apostolic origin. This has been proved a long time since, to every unbiased spirit " (p. 179).

The ordinary creed professed when Protestants joined the Roman Catholic Church, and which is called the Profession of Converts, has these sentences: " I also profess that there are seven sacraments instituted by Jesus Christ our Lord, and necessary for the salvation of mankind." " I do freely profess and hold the true catholic faith, without which no salvation is possible."

Whatever amiable Roman Catholics may think, the Church officially dooms all non-Roman Catholics to destruction. On this point further, is the enactment of the Council of Trent, " If any shall say that the Holy Spirit is not given by holy ordination, let him be accursed. If any shall say that in the New Testament there is no visible and outward priesthood, or that it has not any power of consecration and offering the true body and blood of the Lord, and of remitting and retaining sins, but that it is a mere office and bare ministry of preaching the gospel, let him be accursed."

A PARTIAL BIBLIOGRAPHY

ALLEN, A. V. G., Christian Institutions, New York, Scribners, 1906.

A LAYMAN, Essays on the Church, London, 1840.

BACHOFFEN, CHARLES, L'Ecclesiologie de Zwingle, Geneve, 1890.

BANNERMAN, D. D., Scripture Doctrine of the Church, Edinburgh, 1887.

BENEZECH, ALFRED, La Lutte contra le clericalisme, Fischbacher, Paris, 1903.

BOARDMAN, G. D., The Church (Ecclesia), New York, 1901.

BROWN, JOHN, Apostolical Succession, London, 1898.

BRUCE, R., Apostolic Order and Unity, Edinburgh, 1903 (An Anglican Canon, opposing apostolic succession).

BOYD–CARPENTER, W., Thoughts on Christian Reunion, Macmillan, 1902.

CHAPMAN, JOHN (Reply to), Bishop Gore and Catholic Claims, Longmans, Green & Co., London, 1905.

CHRIST AND THE CHURCH, Essays, New York, 1895.

COLEMAN, LYMAN, Manual on Prelacy and Ritualism, Lippincott, 1869.

COLEMAN, LYMAN, Apostolic and Primitive Church, Boston, 1844.

DALE, R. W., Jewish Temple and Christian Church, London, 1886.

DELITZSCH, F., Vier Buecher von der Kirche, Dresden, 1847.

DICTIONARY of Christian Biography, Smith & Wace, Boston, 1877.

DIECKHOFF, WILHELM, Zur Lehre vom Kirch enregimente. Theolog. Zeitschrift, IV : 481–539, 682–767.

DORNER, A., Kirche und Reichgottes, Gotha, 1883.

DURELL, J. G. V., The Historic Church, Cambridge, 1906. (High-church view-point.)

DYKES, J. O., Anglican View of the Church, Presbyterian Board, Philadelphia, 1897. (A short essay against high-church Anglicanism.)

EDGAR, SAMUEL, Variations of Popery, New York, 1849. (Contains much original matter and a valuable bibliography of Roman Catholic authorities.)

ENGLISH AUTHORS, Our Churches, Why We Belong to Them, Service & Paton, London, 1898.

FEUERBACH, FRIEDRICH, Kirche der Zukunft, Berne, 1847.

FISHER, G. P., Non-Prelatical Ordination, Philadelphia, 1897.

FOSTER, FRANK H., Fundamental Ideas of the Roman Catholic Church, Philadelphia, 1899. (Contains much valuable matter.)

GALLAGHER, MASON, Was the Apostle Peter ever at Rome, New York, 1894.

GALLAGHER, MASON, The True Historical Episcopate, New York, 1890.

GARDNER, PERCY, Growth of Christianity, London Lectures, London, 1907. (Chapter VII deals specifically with the Catholic-Roman Church. Chapter X is on Development. The whole written from a liberal point of view.)

GASPARIN, A., L'Eglise selon l'Evangile, Paris, 1882.

GAYFORD, S. C., Hastings Dict., Article " Church."

GIBBONS, JAMES, Faith of Our Fathers, Baltimore and London, 1895.

GLADSTONE, W. E., Church Principles in Results, 1840.

GROSCLAUDE, CHARLES, L'Ecclesiologie de Calvin, Geneve, 1896.

GOODE, W., Vindication of the Doctrine of the Church of England on Validity of Orders of Scotch and Foreign non-Episcopal Churches, 1852.

GORE, CHARLES, The Church and Ministry, London, 1900. (Only this volume is quoted in the present writing.)

GORE, CHARLES, Mission of the Church, Scribners, 1892.

GOULBURN, Dean of Norwich, The Holy Catholic Church, Pott, Young & Co., 1873.

GWATKIN, H. M., Hastings Dictionary, article " Apostle."

HARLESS, C. A., Kirche und Amt (with reference to Luther's utterances), Stuttgart, 1853.

HARNACK, A., Chronologie der alt-Christlichen Literature, 1897.

HARNACK, A., Texte und Untersuchungen II, Chapters I, II, V.

HARNACK, A., History of Dogma, Boston, 1895-1900.

HASTINGS, ROSS A., The Church-Kingdom, Boston and Chicago, Congregational Publication Society.

HATCH, EDWIN, Growth of Christian Institutions, Hodder & Stoughton, 1888.

HATCH, EDWIN, Organization of Early Christian Churches, 1880.

HENSON, H. H., Apostolic Christianity, Methuen & Co., London, 1898. (Liberal Anglican opinion represented.)

HODGE, CHARLES, Church Polity, New York, 1878. (One of the most valuable books on the Church.)

HOENIG, WILHELM, Katholische und Protestantische Kirchenbegriff in ihren geschichtlichen Entwickelung, Berlin, 1894.

HOPKINS, S., Manual of Church Polity, Auburn, 1878.

HORT, F. J. A., The Christian Ecclesia, London, 1879.

HUNTINGTON, W. D., Peace of the Church, New York, 1893.

HUSSEY, R., Rise of Papal Power, Oxford, 1863. (Valuable material on this subject.)

HUTTON, ARTHUR W., Anglican Ministry, Its Nature and Value in Relation to the Catholic Priesthood, London, 1879. (Severe criticism of the Anglican Catholic claims.)

HUTTON, R. H., Essays, Theological, London, Macmillan, 1880.

KENRICK, F. P., Vindication of

the Catholic Church, Baltimore, 1855.

KETTLEWELL, SAMUEL, Inquiry into the Basis of True Christian Unity, London, 1888.

KILLEN, W. D., The Framework of the Church, Edinburgh, 1890. (Represents high-church presbyterianism.)

KOESTLIN, J., Das Wesen der Kirchenach Lehre und Gesch. des N. T., 1872.

KUEHL, ERNST, Gemeindeordnung, Berlin, 1885.

KUHL, WM., Kirchenrechts und Kirchen politik, Leipzig, 1894. (Especially pp. 118 ff.)

LIGHTFOOT, J. B., Essay on Christian Ministry, Commentary on Philippians, 1868.

LINDSAY, T. M., Church and Ministry in the Early Centuries, New York and London, 1902.

LOENING, EDGAR, Gemeindeverfassung des Urchristenthums, 1889.

LOISY, A., Gospel and Church (English translation), New York, 1904.

LOOFS, FR., Studien und Kritiken, 1890.

LOWRIE, WALTER, The Church and Its Organization in Primitive and Catholic Times, New York, 1904.

MAILHET, ALBERT, Notion de l'Eglise dans Calvin, Montauban, 1881.

MANNING, H. E., The Unity of the Church, London, 1842, New York, 1844.

MARTINEAU, JAMES, Seat of Authority in Religion, London, 1890.

MASON, A. J., The Faith of the Gospel, New York, 1903.

MASON, A. J., Principles of Ecclesiastical Unity, 1896. (Highchurch Anglican.)

MAURICE, F. D., Kingdom of Christ, Appleton, 1843.

McGIFFERT, A. C., Apostolic Age, Scribners, 1897.

MOBERLY, R. C., Ministerial Priesthood, New York, 1898.

MOEHLER, JOHN ADAM, Symbolism; or Exposition of the Doctrinal Differences between Catholics and Protestants, 2 Vols., 2d Ed., London, 1847, Scribners, 1906.

MORRIS, EDWARD D., Ecclesiology, Scribners, 1885.

MUENCHMEYER, A. F., Das Dogma von der Sichtbaren und Unsichtbaren Kirche, Göttingen, 1854.

MYERS, FREDERICK, Catholic Thoughts on the Church of England, London, 1878. (A truly Catholic view of the Church.)

NEALE, J. M., The Church and the Churches.

NEALE, J. M., History of the Holy Eastern Church, London, 1850.

NEANDER, A., History of the Planting and Training of the Christian Church (Eng.), 1851.

OMAN, JOHN, Problem of Faith and Freedom, New York, 1906.

PALMER, WM., Church of Christ, Oxford, 1838.

PECK, T. E., Ecclesiology, Richmond, Va., 1892.

PETERSEN, AUGUST, Die Idee der Christlichen Kirche, Leipzig, 1839.

PULLER, F. W., Primitive Saints

and the See of Rome, 3d Ed., London and New York, 1900.

RAMSAY, W. M., The Church in the Roman Empire, New York, 1893.

RAUSCH, ERWIN, Kirche und Kirchen im Lichte griechischer Forschung, Naumburg, 1901.

RÉVILLE, A., Les Origines de l'Episcopat (1894).

RIGGS, J., Comparative View of Church Organization, London, 1887. (Wesleyan view-point.)

RITSCHL, A., Entstehung der Altkatholischen Kirche.

RITSCHL, A., Rechtfertigung und versohung.

ROBERTSON, A. (Bishop of Exeter), Bampton Lectures, 1901. Regnum Dei, London and New York, 1901.

ROHNERT, WM., Kirchen und Sekten, Leipzig, 1900.

SABATIER, A., Religions of Authority (English translation), 1904. (See the Valuable Appendix.)

SANDAY, W., Conception of Priesthood, 1898.

SANDERSON, J., What is the Church, London, 1897.

SATTERLEE, H. Y., New Testament Churchmanship, Longmans, 1899.

SCHMIEDEL, P. W., Ency. Bibl., articles "Ministry" and "Community of Goods."

SCHAFF, P., Creeds of Christendom, New York, 1877.

SEEBERG, R., Der Begriff der Christlichen Kirche, 1887.

SMYTH'S, THOMAS, Lectures on Apostolical Succession, The Prelatical Doctrine of, examined, Boston, 1841.

SOHM, R., Kirchenrecht, Leipzig, 1892, Band I.

STANLEY, A. P., Christian Institutions, New York, 1881.

STONE, DARWELL, The Christian Church, Rivingtons, 1905. (Valuable material; written from high-church point of view.)

STONE, DARWELL, The Church, Its Ministry and Authority, Rivingtons, 1902.

TYRRELL, GEORGE, The Church of Christ, Methuen & Co., London, 1902, Lex Orandi, London, 1903. (Liberal Roman Catholic.)

VAN DYKE, H. J., The Church, Her Ministry and Sacraments, New York, 1890. (Broad Presbyterian view-point.)

VOS, G., Teaching of Jesus Concerning the Kingdom and Church, New York, 1903.

WACE, HENRY (Editor of), Appeal to the First Six Centuries, London, 1905.

WARD, J. H., Church in Modern Society, Houghton & Mifflin, 1889.

WEINEL, HEINRICH, Paulus als Kirchlicher Organisator, Freiburg, 1899.

WEIZSÄCKER, CARL, The Apostolic Age (English translation), London, 1899.

WENDT, B., Zwei Bucher, v. d. Kirche, Halle, 1859.

WHATELY, RICHARD, Kingdom of Christ, London, 1842.

WISEMAN, NICHOLAS, Conferences sur l'Eglise, et sur divers articles de la Foi Catholique (Traduit), Tours, 1840.

WITHEROW, THOS., Form of Christian Temple, Scribners, 1889.

INDEX OF NAMES AND SUBJECTS

(Numbers refer to pages)

INDEX OF TEXTS

(Pages in parentheses)

Psalm 74 : 2 (84) ; 22 : 23 (80)
Jeremiah 31 : 1 (105) ; 31 : 32 (105) ; 32 : 37 (105)
Matt. 16 : 18 (79, 84, 109, 118, 119) ; 18 : 17 (81) ; 21 : 42 (118)
Mark 3 : 14 (127)
Luke 10 : 1 (127) ; 10 : 30 (150)
John 7 : 38 (139) ; 9 : 34 (111) ; 10 : 16 (109) ; 11 : 52 (109) ; 17 : 6 (270) ; 20 : 21 (127) ; 20 : 23 (119)
Acts 1 : 15–26 (126) ; 1 : 13–15 (128) ; 1 : 16 (129) ; 2 : 42 (226) ; 2 : 47 (75, 90) ; 5 : 11 (83) ; 6 : 6 (140) ; 7 : 38 (109, 271) ; 7 : 38 (81) ; 8 : 1 (83, 133) ; 8 : 3 (83) ; 9 : 2 (81) ; 9 : 42 (90, 248) ; 13 : 1 (131) ; 13 : 13 (141) ; 14 : 2–3 (138) ; 15 : 1 (135) ; 15 : 6 (22) ; 15 : 3 (83) ; 16 : 3 (159) ; 19 : 32, 39, 41 (81) ; 20 : 17–35 (162) ; 20 : 8 (84) ; 20 : 28 (87) ; 22 : 4 (90) ; 24 : 14 (90) ; 24 : 17 (244)
Romans 1 : 7 (91) ; 2 : 27 (74) ; 11 : 12 (112) ; 12 : 1 (241, 244) ; 12 : 3 (254) ; 12 : 6 (255) ; 12 : 6–8 (137) ; 15 : 16 (244) ; 16 : 1–3 (160) ; 16 : 16 (103) ; 16 : 17 (226)
1 Corinthians 1 : 2 (83, 87, 90, 92, 224) ; 1 : 11 (226) ; 3 : 5 (162) ; 4 : 14–17 (225) ; 4 : 15 (136) ; 5 : 9 (226) ; 6 : 11 (90) ; 7 : 17 (225) ; 10 : 16 (85, 103, 225) ; 11 : 18 (82) ; 11 : 22 (87) ; 12 : 7 (254) ; 12 : 28 (137) ; 12 : 8–10 (255) ; 12 : 25 (263) ; 14 : 4 (82) ; 14 : 19 (82) ; 14 : 33, 36 (225) ; 15 : 5 (130) ; 15 : 15 (130) ; 16 : 1 (225) ; 16 : 15 (165, 263) ; 16 : 16 (85) ; 16 : 17 (226) ; 16 : 19 (85)
2 Corinthians 1 : 1 (83, 91) ; 6 : 4–7 (239) ; 6 : 16 (93) ; 6 : 17 (107) ; 7 : 9 (226) ; 10 : 4 (239) ; 11 : 2 (93)
Galatians 1 : 2 (85, 91) ; 1 : 22 (85) ; 3 : 16 (108) ; 3 : 26 (108) ; 4 : 4 (286) ; 6 : 1 (226)
Ephesians 5 : 23–32 (103) ; 2 : 20 (119) ; 3 : 7 (162) ; 4 : 2 (227) ; 4 : 11 (137) ; 4 : 13 (284)
Philippians 1 : 1 (138) ; 1 : 5 (226) ; 2 : 1 (226) ; 4 : 18 (244)
Colossians 1 : 24 (162)
1 Thessalonians 1 : 1 (90) ; 2 : 14 (82, 90) ; 1 : 3 (92) ; 2 : 14 (103) ; 2 : 11 (136) ; 2 : 19 (230) ; 5 : 12 (138) ; 3 : 2 (162)
2 Thess. 3 : 14 (226)
1 Timothy 3 : 13 (163) ; 3 : 15 (93) ; 2 : 11 (108) ; 5 : 17 (138) ; 5 : 22 (141) ; 4 : 14 (141)
2 Timothy 1 : 6 (141)
Titus 2 : 11 (108) ; 3 : 10 (226)
Hebrews 2 : 12 (80) ; 3 : 1–6 (84) ; 3 : 5 (271) ; 3 : 6 (93) ; Chapters 8, 9, 10 (107) ; 10 : 25 (80) ; 7 : 14 (149) ; 12 : 23 (269) ; 13 : 23 (226)
James 2 : 2 (80) ; 13 : 15 (244)
1 Peter 2 : 4–6 (118) ; 2 : 5 (244)
2 Peter 3 : 18 (284)
Revelation 2 : 9 (80) ; 3 : 9 (80) ; 6 : 2 (270) ; 12 : 1 (286)

319